NEW ORGANIZATIONS FROM OLD

Derek Taylor worked on R & D as a physicist with ICI Ltd before joining the Operational Research Group of the National Coal Board to assist in developing policy at national and colliery level. Later as a consultant, first with H B Maynard & Co Inc of Pittsburg, USA, and then with Coopers & Lybrand Associates Ltd, he carried out assignments in the USA, Sweden, Switzerland and the UK concerned with restructuring organizations and improving the business performance of companies in light engineering, industrial instrumentation, television rental and insurance. He also helped the Government of Jersey, Channel Islands, to reorganize their Civil Service, the Post Office and the Milk Marketing Board. He also assisted the Government of Guernsey in setting up an agency for planning the island's economic development. In between these two consulting appointments he had some years experience of general management as Managing Director of English Velvets Ltd, a group of six textile companies, with the responsibility for carrying out a salvage operation on the group.

In 1973 he joined the Scandinavian Institute for Administrative Research (SIAR) in Sweden during which time he specialized in strategic planning and organizational development.

He is presently Director of Management and Business Development at Kingston Regional Management Centre where his main interests lie in assisting organizations to learn how to cope with today's changing and uncertain environment. He is currently a member of the executive committee of the Society for Strategic and Long Range Planning and advisor on strategic planning and organizational issues to the Crown Agents for Overseas Governments and Administrations and to Control Data Ltd.

Edwin Singer has run his own consultancy since 1972, after being a senior consultant with Urwick, Orr and Partners. He has a lifetime's experience of working in industry, commerce and public bodies. He has extensive experience of the education system and has been closely connected with various aspects of the development of youth training provision in the UK.

Currently he is an Industrial Fellow at Kingston Regional Management Centre, Secretary of the Centre for Learning and Development, a Director of the Windsor Consulting Group, a Member of the IPM's National Committee for Training and Development, a Member of the BACIE Council and of its Training Policy Committee. He is the author of a number of books and is well known as a contributor to professional journals and as a speaker.

NEW ORGANIZATIONS FROM OLD
How to survive and prosper in a changing environment

Derek E Taylor
Edwin J Singer

Institute of Personnel Management
IPM House, 35 Camp Road, Wimbledon, London SW19 4OW

This book is dedicated to the late Dr Charles Frankland Moore OBE, LLD, FIMechE, CEng, a most informed and helpful man

© Institute of Personnel Management 1983
First published 1983

All rights reserved. No part of this publication may be reproduced, stored in a retrieval system, or transmitted in any form or by any means, electronic, mechanical, photocopying, recording or otherwise, without written permission of
The Institute of Personnel Management,
IPM House, Camp Road,
Wimbledon, London sw19 4uw

Text set in 11/12pt Linotron 202 Sabon, printed and bound in Great Britain at The Pitman Press, Bath

British Library Cataloguing in Publication Data
Taylor, Derek E
New organizations from old
1. Organizational change 2. Industrial management
I. Title   II. Singer, Edwin J
658·4'06   HD 58·8
ISBN 0-85292-328-7

Foreword

There could hardly be a more opportune time than now for the publication of this book. The present prolonged recession has forced many companies to accept the need for fundamental structural change; belatedly they have realised that trading conditions will not revert to the status quo ante. I find more and more companies confirming that, when an upturn in the economy occurs and order books do improve, they will still need to remain permanently a lower cost operation.

It is interesting to reflect on how many companies could – and perhaps should – have anticipated the need for the structural change forced on them by the recession. There are a few examples of companies which have adapted to change in a timely and orderly manner, taken the initiative and maintained it; they are, however, few indeed in number. This book, if available earlier, might well have helped to increase the numbers of those skillful few. Being sensitive to the need for change, being aware of the significance of external factors and their potential impact on your business, and not living in market isolation, all need conscious organized effort and thought. If this recession has taught us anything, it is the importance of total commitment and understanding within an organization to the need for change. Without it, the acceptance of change and the will to change and adapt will be delayed and management's tasks frustrated.

I trust readers of this book will find it provoking and constructive, and helpful in deciding how to tackle the vital issue of being responsive to external factors which shape and influence a business.

Sir John Cuckney

'One must never lose time in vainly regretting the past or in complaining against the changes which cause us discomfort, for change is the very essence of life.'

Anatole France

Contents

Foreword	v
Preface	1
Introduction	3
1 Coping with change	7
2 Simulating the natural change process	17
3 Organizations can learn	30
4 How to manage a company's learning	42
5 Strategic planning as a process of learning and change	57
6 Barriers and aids to success	66
7 The change agents	89
8 How one company learned to cope	105
9 Initiating the change process	123
Appendix Getting to know the business and its problems	135
Bibliography	143
Index	149

Preface

This book results from the authors' experiences of helping many organizations to cope effectively with demands made on them by major economic, social, political or technological changes.

Although the book deals mainly with companies engaged in business activities some of the relevant experience has been gained from other types of organization, including government, local government and other parts of the public sector. The problems addressed in the book are common to all of them. Moreover, although the detailed steps required to effect the necessary internal changes may differ, the overall approach described in the following chapters can be used effectively in all these kinds of organization.

Not all the attempts made by the authors to help organizations to deal more effectively with the pressures and new demands created by today's changing world have been successful. Where success has been achieved it has always happened because a sufficient number of people in the organization concerned have developed a different perception of their external world and have both seen the need to and have learned to behave differently as a result of this. Failures have more often than not occurred when perhaps one person has 'seen the light' and then attempted to impose his 'solution' on others without their prior commitment.

The task of writing the book has been complicated by problems of semantics. People attach many different meanings to some of the words used frequently in this work such as organization, strategy, learning, reality etc. Nevertheless, we hope we have been sufficiently precise in our use of these words to convey enough of our meaning. We have been guilty in places of using the words 'company' and 'organization' interchangeably, but hope that this will not create too many problems for the reader.

We wish to thank many people. The works and ideas of Eric Rhenman, formerly of Lund University and Harvard Business School, of Richard Normann now of the Service Management Group AB and of Arthur Johnston of ICI Limited, have all been helpful.

The support of three highly successful entrepreneurs who were also leaders of complex organizations, namely Charles Frankland Moore, Demetrius Comino, and Senator Cyril le Marquand of the State of Jersey was available when needed. Sir John Cuckney, whose present appointments include Chairman of both the Thomas Cook Group and Brooke Bond Liebig plc and Major-General Horace Birks gave encouragement at an early stage in the production of the book.

Sir Sidney Eburne, Alan Frood, Michael Walsh and many others of the Crown Agents, Peter Lucas, formerly of Crown Agents, Eric Bates of the Department of Industry, Tom Maynard former Chief Economist of National Westminster Bank Limited, John Townsend of the Business Education Council, Ian Hinton of the Kingston Regional Management Centre, Gabor Bruszt of SIAR, Edward Potter, Colin Powell and Ron Gray all of the Civil Service of Jersey, CI, Signor Liberati, Alessandro Sinatra and Gianmario Molteni of Dalmine SpA, Fred Mobbs and many others of Control Data Limited, Jack Ward of Worldtech Ventures Limited, David Dey of IBM (Europe), Neil Spoonley of Business Advisers Ltd, Harry Leach and Arthur Barlow of Tootal Limited and Pat Norcross have all contributed in some way.

Thanks are also due to Hano Johannssen and Pat Foulkes of the BIM and George Barber who brought their clear-sighted and constructive criticism to bear on earlier versions of the manuscript.

Thanks are particularly due to our wives Pam Taylor and Rhiannon Singer for the encouragement they gave when this was most needed.

Introduction

Organizations are being subjected constantly to new demands which require them to make significant changes in the way they behave or relate to their surroundings. In the main these demands arise because of major changes (political, social, economic or technological) which take place in the world in which they operate.

This book is about how organizations and their senior executives can learn how to cope with these changes in a way which will enhance the company's chances of survival and show an improvement in its profit performance. Extensive use is made of the words 'learn' and 'learning' in the book so that a few words of explanation of what is meant by them will avoid misunderstanding.

By learning we mean much more than the mere acquisition of knowledge. Real learning has taken place when the new knowledge has been translated into practice. This inevitably means that there have been changes: that people in the organization have stopped doing some things and started doing other, and more relevant, activities which will benefit the company. Learning, therefore, is the process of using the time available in a different, and potentially more profitable, way.

Some managing directors may still ask 'Why should I be interested in "learning"?' It is possible to hire consultants to suggest what should be done; or lay off staff in order to contain costs; or initiate a drive on quality or stock reduction, or speed up work in progress. These are the traditional methods of coping with changing circumstances and to a large extent presuppose that things will get better, or return to normal as part of the traditional business cycle. Our thesis is that the pace of change, and the nature of the forces which impinge on company performance, indicate that we are going through a period of qualitative, as opposed to quantitative, change.

Think, for example, of the future possible patterns of work, the likely levels of unemployment, the influence on world trading patterns of the countries of the third world, or the future price of energy. All these and many other developments lead one to suppose an uncertain future, but a future which is unlikely to be a repetition of the past. Orderly transition to whatever the future holds will demand changed patterns of operating. To determine which pattern should evolve for a particular organization demands not only that it should acquire knowledge and facts, but also think through how new patterns should operate and then give effect to the decisions. For us, this total process is best described as 'learning'.

Few organizations, if any, are so insulated from their environment that they can afford to ignore the various changes which are taking place and the problems they create. It is surprising that the companies which often experience the greatest difficulties are those which at one time were highly successful. Think, for example, of Rolls Royce which survived only after a traumatic period of change during which the company, at one stage, was declared bankrupt. Government departments and agencies are also affected by the changed demands which are sweeping through society. They are expected to be cost effective to a greater extent than ever before as the community begins to question the value it receives from the huge sums of money which it provides for the public sector of the economy.

The problem of learning to adapt to this new type of environment is, therefore, one which faces all types of organization. It may require an organization to make significant changes to what it does and for whom and in how it does it. Furthermore, society has many ways of taking sanctions against any organizations which fail to make the necessary adjustments, from refusing to buy a company's products in sufficient quantities to taking legal action against infringements of laws governing say, pollution.

Although one of the key tasks of management has always been to cope with changing conditions, the magnitude of the transition which organizations now have to make, and the speed with which they are required to make changes, demands that managers acquire new skills.

Some organizations are extremely successful in making the necessary transitions. Such organizations, in fact, appear to have some natural process at work which helps them to recognize the need for change and adapt as necessary. Other organizations are less successful and the gap between what they are and what they should be continues to widen with the passage of time. Others fail completely and in consequence do not survive.

Although the problem of coping with a changing environment is one which faces all types of organization, our concern in this book is mainly with business enterprises of various kinds, though we have not hesitated to draw on the experience of other types of organization. The theme of the book is *New Organizations from Old.* As the pace of change quickens so the gulf between an organization and the environment it seeks to serve is likely to grow. The book is directed at those companies which recognize that there is a gap between what they are doing now and what the outside world is now demanding of them, ie that they are no longer in touch with their business environment.

The aims of the book are to:

(a) draw attention to the fact that this is a problem which is affecting many companies today
(b) create a better understanding of what is involved in getting in tune with a changed and changing environment
(c) explore some of the ways of approaching the problem, emphasizing the importance of the existence in a company of a process which combines both individual and organizational learning
(d) describe such a learning process and explain how it can be managed
(e) discuss the characteristics which top management and change agents need in order to effect the necessary changes.

The book is addressed to chief executives and all other managers who have to deal with problems of this kind. It is also written for the various types of specialist who may assist in this work, such as corporate planners, specialists in management and organizational development, and professional management consultants. It should also be useful for teachers concerned with management education since the task of dealing with the problems of working in a constantly changing environment is one which now confronts all managers. It is not concerned with a set of rules, nor is it about yet another technique, panacea or flavour of the month. It is not a new theory but shows how to put existing theories into practice. Above all, it is based on practical experience.

1
Coping with change

There is nothing new about change, it has been causing 'progress', disruption, fear, adaptation and even enthusiasm since time immemorial. Today we are perhaps more sophisticated about change. We try to anticipate it; discuss it, participate in it and make provision to cushion its effects. In spite of all that, we often resist it to such an extent that when the inevitable takes place and we find ourselves unable to resist any longer, we may well have thrown away the chance to ameliorate its effects.

One main theme of this book is 'coming to terms with reality'. Its message is that organizations are as strong, capable and adaptable as the people who work in them; they need to be in accord with the environment in which they operate and should take account of the expectations of those who work for them without jeopardizing their principal role of providing goods and services at a satisfactory rate of profit. If they fail in this, either the organization will cease to exist or the changes which have been resisted will take place, but with more unpleasant and more far reaching consequences for the people who resisted the change in the first place.

The future business environment will in all probability be turbulent and too uncertain to permit reliance on long-term

forecasts as the basis of future actions. Organizations will have to be capable at short notice of:
1 identifying relevant changes in technology, industry or society as a whole
2 assessing their significance for the company
3 responding appropriately.

Realizing that existing strategies require revision is not easy and doing something about it is even harder. Continuing with what we do well is much easier than launching into the unknown. For one thing, doing something new demands learning, and learning demands extra effort over and above the energies we are already expending on day to day affairs.

How some companies have responded

Keeping a company in tune with its environment is a difficult task, the more so when changes occur in the environment which undermine the very basis of the company's success in the past. For example:

> A well known multiple store company achieved great success by retailing a wide variety of products subject to the policy 'nothing over sixpence'. For a large part of the company's history this strategy matched the spending power of large segments of society during which period the company was extremely successful. The company began to run into difficulties, which it has not yet succeeded in overcoming, when people's spending power increased to the point where they began to look for higher quality products.

Organizations that lose touch with the needs and demands of their environment can respond in various ways, often depending on the size of the gap which has to be narrowed.

Many companies have made major changes in top management in order to introduce into the business a new set of values and different ideas and beliefs about what is needed to change and to improve matters. There are many examples to illustrate this approach. One of the best known occurred when Sir Arnold Weinstock took over the top management role with AEI Ltd. He replaced a set of values more attuned to engineering achievements with one which placed much greater emphasis on short-term profitability. Other examples are provided by Rolls Royce Ltd which was formerly headed by engineers of considerable distinction but which was directed largely by a merchant banker during the period of reconstruction, and also by BL which was put in the hands of Sir Michael Edwardes, who had had no previous experience of the automobile industry.

Success in such cases has usually depended on the soundness of judgment, strength of character and possibly the luck of the new top manager introduced. It is an approach which might be traumatic in its effect on the organization but drastic actions of this kind are often essential for the survival of an enterprise.

Companies have often called on the services of professional management consultants to carry out extensive studies of their organizations, their environments and the effectiveness of the relationships between the two and to recommend ways in which improvements can be made. In the 1960s and early 1970s many well-known organizations followed this course.

This approach has been successful in many cases. However, even where the company's situation has been investigated with considerable skill, projects of this kind can fail because of the consultants' inability to gain acceptance of their recommendations by the people who must implement them. In fact, there must be relatively few consultants engaged in this kind of work who have not experienced partial or complete failures of this kind, usually when they have been unable to influence and to modify the system of attitudes or norms within the organizations concerned.

Organizations have also made attempts to respond to the pressures for change imposed by their environments by initiating programmes based on such activities as management development, management by objectives, team building exercises and structural reorganization of various kinds. Some of these attempts too have failed because many of these interventions have been limited to modifying existing practices rather than introducing more fundamental changes.

Some companies introduced corporate planning as a means of guiding their future development. However, this is an activity which is often confined to one or two individuals who prepare plans which are then largely ignored by the groups in the company who wield real power.

Many companies, even the ones which have engaged in strategic planning for some considerable time, still regard planning as a functional activity to be carried out by a staff solely appointed for this purpose. The main outputs from planners in this situation may tend to be pious statements about what should be done rather than of positive intentions which the company is committed to implement.

A subsidiary of a well known tobacco company employed a small team of specialists to formulate a plan for the future development of the business. Although it was based on an exhaustive analysis of available market, financial and manufacturing information, the preparation of the plan was divorced from the managers who would have to implement it. Consequently, they were not committed to the plan which, in fact, had little influence on the subsequent development of the company.

In other cases companies prepare effective plans for markets and products but neglect to develop related plans and policies for personnel, research and development, finance and production.

Corporate planning as presently carried out, even in companies in which the planning is comprehensive and is allowed to exert influence on the decisions made by senior management, can, however, provide only partial answers to the task of coping successfully with the changing business environment.

Since the pace of change is now often so rapid, organizations need to respond quickly to the changes which occur. The structure, policies and practices of departmental activities such as personnel, production and sales may have to alter fundamentally within a relatively short span of time and in ways which demand different behaviour from people at all levels within those functions. Suggestions for improving strategies made by specialists paid to consider such issues can help, but in the long run changes in the behaviour of the enterprise as a whole or in part can be effected only if the attitudes and behaviour of individuals and groups at many levels in the organization also change.

Clearly, this is a task beyond the function of corporate planning as presently practised in the majority of companies. Although such planning makes new information and ideas available to an organization, it more often than not fails to influence the attitudes, beliefs and values on which commitment to the plan on the part of those who must implement it depends.

The natural process of change

All companies to some extent have the capability of adapting to the changing needs of their environments. There appears to be a natural evolutionary process of change at work which indeed is highly developed in the more successful companies.

This process has been studied by many observers of organizational behaviour and appears to consist of four stages:

1 Developing concern and learning about the situation

The first step is the development of concern somewhere in the organization resulting from a belief that something is not as it should be. This concern invariably arises from some significant mismatch developing in what has previously been a satisfactory relationship between the organization and some part of the environment. Usually, one or two members of the firm will sense that something is wrong and try to alert their colleagues to this in some way or another. Their initial attempts to arouse concern might be, and often are, rejected, particularly where they conflict with well established organizational beliefs and practices.

As the impact of the mismatch on the organization increases, small groups of people with a shared concern begin to form and start to learn more about the basic issues involved. They begin to bring pressure to bear on key figures in the power structure in order to get them involved and to get things moving. The time that this takes can, of course, be much reduced if someone in the leading power group is party to this concern from the outset.

Once a key figure in the top management does decide to take action then the process of identifying the real problems underlying any mismatches which have become evident can begin. This can be regarded as an unfreezing process. It is a stage of acceptance and demonstration of the will to change by key members of the power group which is vital if real progress is to be made. It is only when this has occurred that behaviour beyond that which is normally valued by the organization becomes acceptable.

2 Diagnosing and acknowledging the problem

The next stage in the process is the fact finding and diagnosis necessary to develop a real understanding of the problem or problems creating the mismatches already identified. It is essential that a vigorous problem-solving process should be adopted at this stage since there are many ways in which the process can go wrong. There may be a tendency to accept a superficial definition of the problem in order to get it out of the way. The greatest danger exists when the problem embraces some well established norm in the organization where the tendency to 'rationalize' or to blame someone else for what might be going wrong will become all too evident to an impartial observer. Where this is likely to happen it is essential for the key figures supporting the review to show their willingness to commit themselves to what may be a fundamental change in strategy and work practices.

The natural change process is also likely to progress more smoothly if the understanding of the problem situation is shared widely amongst the people who must implement any solution. Usually these people will be part of the problem to be solved, and it is only when this is recognized by them that real problem solving (as distinct from paying 'lip service') will begin to take place. If the change process is to be effective this stage should end with a clear identification of the problems to be solved and the ways suggested of solving them.

3 Taking action

In companies which are most successful in adapting to changing circumstances the solutions chosen are implemented as part of a well managed process. This process involves identifying the implications of the change and planning to ensure that any undesirable impacts on management and staff will be minimized. This helps to counteract any effective resistance developing to the proposed changes, particularly if during the earlier stages of fact finding and diagnosis sufficient attention has been paid to involving the people who in the end are likely to be responsible for implementing change.

4 Stabilizing the changes

Once new strategies or changes in working practices have been introduced the next step is for the organization to legitimize them and to ensure they become a continuing part of future operations. Failure in this respect may well lead to a relapse to old and more familiar methods!

In order to stabilize the changes it is usually necessary to ensure that the important organizational characteristics, such as the system of rewards and punishments, information and control systems and the distribution of power, authority and status, are modified to reinforce the new organizational behaviour.

WHERE THE NATURAL PROCESS FAILS

As discussed, the natural process of change is one which operates successfully in those companies which can respond rapidly and effectively to environmental changes.

Resistance to change is inherent in any organization. People become used to established beliefs, policies and procedures and can feel threatened if any attempts are made to change them. This is particularly so if the managers concerned:

(a) are not fully convinced of the need for making changes.

In such a case they will invariably attempt to maintain the 'status quo' while paying 'lip service' to an acceptance of changes contemplated

(b) are preoccupied with day to day problems to the exclusion of giving attention to longer term trends. The need to ensure that today's production target is met in spite of sickness, absenteeism or industrial disputes, or the need to handle the complaints of an irate yet important customer can prevent managers from noticing that the company's products are no longer meeting customer needs adequately, let alone taking any action to correct this situation

(c) hold deeply entrenched ideas which are geared to past successes or failures rather than to present circumstances

(d) lack a commitment to the objectives of the enterprise

(e) believe that their power, authority and status will be adversely affected

(f) are reluctant to change methods of working with which they have become familiar

(g) lack the will to change

(h) have been in the company for many years and little new blood, and therefore new ideas, have been introduced into the organization.

In companies where enough of these conditions apply then the natural process will be too attenuated to develop appropriate changes in organizational behaviour. In these cases more drastic steps need to be taken and a formal planned and managed programme of change will need to be introduced which to all intents and purposes will *simulate* the natural process described above.

Changing an established organization in response to external pressures can never be an easy task. Changes, in fact, will take place only if there is sufficient concern in the organization that there is something wrong, and sufficient time is set aside to 'think' and get away from day to day concerns. Moreover, there must be an awareness that whatever is wrong is likely to have an adverse effect on the company's performance, possibly to the extent of threatening the well-being of the organization as a whole or some important part of it.

It is not the intention at this stage to spell out the details of what is needed to simulate the natural process of change. It is useful, however, to identify some of the key requirements of such a process.

The first requirement for an organization which hopes to make a successful 'transition' from being out of touch with its environment to a position of strength, is the presence in top management of someone who is prepared to examine in detail the problems involved in effecting major changes and exploring the steps which need to be taken if the changes are to achieve acceptable results. It must be a person who on the one hand appreciates the relevance of new knowledge and up to date ideas and beliefs in effecting the transition, and on the other has the power to initiate and progress an appropriate programme of education and learning to achieve this end. More importantly, he/she must possess both the wish and the will to initiate and progress any changes which are necessary, and must be prepared to be relentless in their pursuit. He must in fact be prepared to become the major driving force behind the change process.

Since a company may have to make many significant changes in what it does and for whom and how it does it, this will not be achieved without a great deal of learning taking place. Managers will almost certainly have to learn a great deal about the changes required in order to continue to achieve the company's goals. The company will also need the ability to respond to what it has learned. It is this process of learning which enables an organization to change or to adapt itself to meet the needs of a changing environment.

The learning needs will almost certainly be different for enterprises at different stages of growth and maturity. The longer established and more mature organization which has grown out of touch with the changing needs of its customers, clients, suppliers or other interested parties has many problems to solve. The process needed requires that some way must be found to challenge successfully and to discard, or perhaps ignore, existing ideas, beliefs and values before new knowledge and understanding can be gained and working practices adjusted. It requires a process of regeneration rather than simply one of growth. It is not enough that individuals in the company should learn; the organization itself also needs to learn. This means that a sufficiently influential group of managers must demonstrate a willingness to introduce and to accept change. The learning required is of the kind which can lead to:

(a) significant changes in the prevailing ideas, beliefs and values held in key parts of the organization
(b) the acquisition of new forms of organizational behaviour.

It means that the right people and groups of people must be learning about the right things. Those who can, in fact, initiate change must learn to identify and to solve the new problems created by the changing environmental demands and expectations. Those who can inhibit change must learn about the inadequacies of their existing attitudes and methods of working. It may require a greater capacity for learning than many organizations currently possess.

The process which makes this kind of learning possible has implications for the ways in which organizations are structured, for the nature and extent of their data-bases and for their information and control systems. Particularly important is the extent to which people at all levels need to participate in the collection and analysis of information and in problem solving, decision making and feedback processes.

A third requirement is the presence in the organization of one or more persons who can act as effective catalysts or 'change agents' in helping to bring about the transition. These agents may be either internal or external to the organization itself providing they have the necessary knowledge and skills and are given sufficient freedom to act. Experience has shown that a team composed of a chief executive working with an external adviser, and someone within the organization who has the freedom to relate to, and communicate with, all levels of management, can be extremely effective in conducting a major programme of organizational change.

2
Simulating the natural change process

Simulating the natural process of change depends first on identifying those things which are preventing the company being as successful as it might be and secondly on finding the means to overcome those obstacles.

What constitutes a successful company? Experience suggests that a company can usually be regarded as successful when there is congruence between the company's environment, its situation in that environment, its organization and the strategies it is employing, and its values and norms, ie between the groups of factors represented by the three circles in figure 1 below. If there are serious mismatches between these groups of factors the company will be less successful than it might otherwise be.

Consequently, a company can generally be made more effective by identifying and eliminating any mismatches which are found to exist. An analysis leading to their identification and the diagnosis of what causes them can, therefore, be an important step in the change process required to help a company cope or to realign itself with its environment. Such an analysis will usually require a detailed examination of the groups of factors represented by the three circles in figure 1 namely:

1 the company's environment and its situation in relation to it

2 the company's organization and the strategies it is employing
3 the company's system of ideas, beliefs, values and norms.

Figure 1

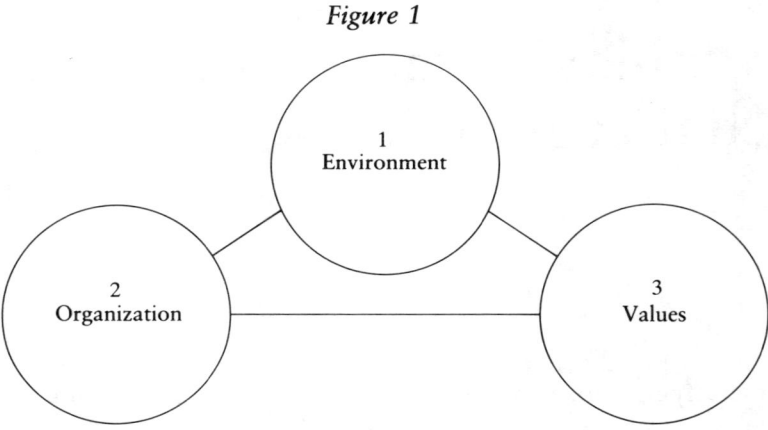

THE COMPANY'S ENVIRONMENT AND ITS POSITION IN RELATION TO IT

The way in which a company adapts in order to exploit its environment will depend partly on the profit and growth objectives it seeks to achieve and partly on its existing position in relation to its own particular environment. For example, consider two companies which have similar growth and profit objectives, but whose situations are appreciably different.

Company A

Company A has a limited range of products which it sells to a restricted market in which it has greater than 50 per cent share and thus dominates the market in question. The company has obtained its dominant market share by developing a special competence based on superior products and a way of marketing and distributing them which has given it a distinct advantage over its competitors. Since the market is now saturated and is not growing in size the company, to achieve growth objectives, needs to adopt a strategy of diversification, either in terms of new products in existing markets, existing products in new markets, new products in new markets, or possibly by takeover or merger, whichever it finds to be most appropriate.

Company B

Company B on the other hand is operating in many different markets with an extensive range of products. It has only a limited share of each market in which it is engaged and does not have the necessary competence in any of them to dominate or make much money from them. Although it has achieved growth in turnover by virtue of working in many different directions its profits have not increased accordingly. The strategy required here is to concentrate on the markets where the company is more likely to develop some distinctive competence in relation to its competitors.

The importance of understanding a company's true situation in relation to its environment, bearing in mind that the environment itself may be changing rapidly, is paramount when developing effective strategies. Failure to do so may lead to the adoption of inappropriate strategies or their continuation when no longer successful.

The first step in developing that understanding is to identify the individuals, groups or organization which have some form of direct relationship with the company (ie stakeholders, such as customers, suppliers, shareholders, employees, bankers, suppliers of credit, debtors, unions, the labour market and so on). The next step is to determine which needs of these interest groups are being satisfied by the company and what the company is receiving in return. It may be that imbalances exist between what the company is giving and receiving and that therefore there is an urgent need to adjust the balance of benefits.

Although employees are an integral part of an organization they can also be regarded as part of the company's environment in that, like other stakeholders, they make demands on the company which must be satisfied if the company is to remain healthy.

The company also needs to establish a thorough knowledge of such things as:

1 Its existing and potential markets, and its position in them, eg market share, income generated, margins obtained, profits earned, growth potential, whether it is expanding or contracting in these markets and whether the markets themselves are undergoing any expansion or contraction.

2 Its competitors; the market share held by the more significant of them, what they have to offer that is responsible for their success and any distinctive competence or advantage the company itself might have in relation to them.

THE COMPANY'S ORGANIZATION

The term 'organization' is used here to mean the totality of such things as products, services, people, skills, problem-solving capabilities, machines, finance, other fixed assets, processes, production, marketing and other leading systems, etc.

'Organization structure' on the other hand is confined to such things as the shape of the organization, areas of responsibilities, reporting relationships, communications channels, information and control systems such as production and budgetary control, and the way in which these elements are linked together.

The nature of the organization, particularly its strengths and weaknesses in relation to its environment, is highly relevant to the strategies which the company should adopt in order to achieve its objectives.

It is not enough to know the components which together form the organization, it is also important to know how, and how well, they relate to the environment and to one another. For example:

1 it is desirable to know how sales effort is allocated to the company's different market segments and how well this

matches the potential for future profit from the various segments because this helps to achieve profitable utilization of the available sales resources

2 it is important to know whether the company has adequate production capacity for the products to which a major marketing effort is being allocated. If such effort is not specifically directed there is the danger that the company will sell more than it is capable of producing, thereby alienating potential customers

3 it is essential to know where and to what extent working capital is being used in a growing business, otherwise there is the real danger that the company will run into difficulties if the demand for capital to finance the growth exceeds available funds.

THE COMPANY'S SYSTEM OF IDEAS, BELIEFS AND VALUES

Every company has a system of values and norms which are unique to itself. These values are made up partly from the ideas, beliefs, standards and attitudes held by the key people in the company. However, the traditions of the company, built up from its earliest days, are also a source of myth and reality which need to be taken into account if people in the company are to be persuaded to behave differently.

This system of values embodies the ideas in a company of what is good or bad, of what is desirable and what is not and which govern the decision making in the company. It unifies decision making, provides links between the decisions of different people and between decisions made at different times. The value system which embraces company policy also satisfies important psychological needs of the company's employees in their roles as decision makers and helps to provide justification for their actions.

The values concerned will include, for example, ideas and beliefs about such things as:

(a) why the company is in business

(b) why the company is successful or unsuccessful
(c) what is important for success in the industry concerned
(d) how best to exploit the environment
(e) how the company makes its money
(f) how to motivate and manage people
(g) what levels of growth and profit, etc are acceptable
(h) which goals or objectives should be pursued.

Some of these ideas or beliefs will take precedence over or dominate some of the other ideas, particularly where the former are held by key members of the leading power group. They will largely govern how the company behaves. There are, however, usually a number of other power groups at different levels in the company who may have different norms and who can strongly influence what happens in their particular part of the company.

It is obvious that any major inconsistencies between the values held by different key people or by different important power groups can only lead to problems for the company as forces pull in different directions. Consequently it is desirable to strive for harmony between the values of individuals and those of the organization. It is particularly important that those values which form the over-riding goals of the oganization should be widely shared throughout the company otherwise there will be inadequate co-ordination between the activities of different parts of the company.

It is also important that there should be congruence between the company's value system and the values held by important parts of its environment. For example those aspects of the company's products which it considers to be of great significance should match what the customer thinks is important.

Mismatches can contribute to lack of success

As the environment changes there is a tendency for an organization and its value system to become increasingly out of tune with it, and the company's performance will usually deteriorate unless a process of adjustment brings these factors back into congruence.

Many examples of mismatches between the organization and its environment can be cited. One company began to lose business and to incur losses when, largely as a result of lack of investment in new plant and equipment, its methods of manufacture became much less cost effective than those of its competitors. Another company devoted resources to the development of a product group for which demand was static and which failed to expand even with product modification. A third company allocated sales resources to a market which was declining and neglected the opportunities presented by an expanding market in which it was also engaged. It was not long before each company was failing to obtain enough income and adequate margins to generate a profit.

Mismatches will occur if a company fails to exploit its environment and the members of the main power groups hold ideas which are no longer valid about the requirements for success.

> A textile company devoted considerable resources to traditional markets with which members of the leading power group were familiar, but which were no longer profitable. At the same time, they paid less attention to a newer business area from which the company was making much of its money and which had greater profit potential, in both the short and medium term.

A common type of mismatch can occur when a company appoints a senior executive with a value system different from the company's own.

> A mature and successful company manufacturing and installing lighting systems appointed a new and young chief executive. His ambitions for profitable growth led him to set goals which were far higher than those of his predecessor. This imposed demands for change in the company's level of activities, its organization, the markets it was attempting to exploit and its market share requirements. This in turn created further mismatches and difficulties for members of the management team.

A company's system of values can lead to practices which result ultimately in an organization which is no longer competent enough to cope satisfactorily with its environment. The mismatch in this case might be between important aspects of the company's value system and those of its competitors.

The chairman of a group of public companies engaged in heavy engineering consistently filled the most senior appointments with members of his family regardless of the greater competence of other senior executives. In the course of time the company was unable to recruit and keep a sufficiently competent senior management team to maintain satisfactory levels of performance.

Serious mismatches can occur between different parts of a company, for example where differences in departmental objectives can lead to conflict instead of co-operation.

In a company with a functional organization structure which manufactured electronic measuring equipment the production and sales departments had objectives which were in conflict with one another. These were pursued relentlessly, often at the expense of the business as a whole. The production director was concerned with manufacturing as small a range of products as possible, to keep his costs to a minimum; the sales director was keen to offer a wider range of products to the market place, to assist him to achieve his budgeted level of turnover. This inadequately controlled situation resulted in a reduction in profitability and, at the same time, placed the long-term survival of the company at risk.

Mismatches often occur in a company's production system because it has 'grown like Topsy', which can lead to manufacturing costs greatly in excess of what could be achieved. PC Schumacher has, in fact, concluded from a number of projects (designed to restructure work situations) that it is usually possible to reduce the amount of value added to a product in the course of manufacture by at least 30 per cent when the mismatches found in most production systems have been eliminated even though the operations concerned have already been improved by using conventional work study techniques.

Some of the most serious company problems can occur when the system of values of the key power group are out of touch with reality.

A large company in Europe had traditionally manufactured steel tubes of various sizes for many different end uses, including household use. In recent years they set up a subsidiary company manufacturing tube from plastics but as these were considered to be inferior to steel tubing, the subsidiary company never received the support or the level of investment that was justified by the scope for the plastic products. Subsequently, a specialist chemical company saw the potential, started to manufacture the plastic tubing and went on to create a large and profitable business.

A second example of this type of situation is provided by a large conglomerate concerned with high technology products and projects. The chairman had built the company up from scratch using an authoritarian approach to managing and making all major decisions himself. In later years much of the company growth was achieved by taking over smaller firms concerned with high technology which had generally been set up by technically minded entrepreneurs used to making important decisions for themselves. The conflicts which occurred between the chairman's beliefs and approach and those of the newcomers restricted the growth and development of the subsidiaries.

In most companies there are usually a number of other power groups, possibly within departments or sections which can also have significant effects on the behaviour of parts of the organization and whose values may be appreciably different from those of the leading power group.

The top management group of a firm manufacturing hydraulic control systems tried to impose a system of standard costing and budgetary control onto its various cost centres without first gaining the acceptance of the departmental managers. Consequently, although lip service was paid to the system, the departmental managers, who saw it as a threat to their own power, made sure that the system did not work.

Another example in the same company occurred when it began to market a new control instrument basing the price on what senior management assumed to be a conservative estimate of the level of productivity for the instrument in full scale manufacture. This level of productivity was never achieved partly because the managers of the production departments concerned refused to accept it. The instrument which had considerable market potential was finally withdrawn as it continued to lose money.

The greater the diversity and the more the conflicts which exist between the values of the various power groups in the enterprise the less the chance of the enterprise acting as a unified, cohesive and well directed entity. Yet the task of coping with, and competing successfully in, the present changing environment requires that these power groups should work together. They need to act in unison even when all the power groups in question are not in direct contact with the environmental factors which create the need for a change in behaviour.

Profiting from mismatches

Although mismatches occurring between the factors represented by the three circles in figure 1 on page 18 can inhibit profitable growth or otherwise detract from performance, there is a positive aspect to many mismatches. If the problem-solving capability of a company is up to the task, the rectification of a mismatch can lead to further profitable growth and development.

A good example of this is provided by the Timex Corporation in its early days. The company produced a good quality watch at a low price as a result of applying an advanced technology developed during the First World War. At that time the distribution of watches was almost entirely through jewellers who refused to handle what they wrongly regarded as a cheap and inferior product. Faced with this mismatch or barrier to growth, the company's dynamic leader began to market his watches through drugstores and other retail outlets outside the jewellery trade. This strategy proved to be extremely successful and laid the foundations for considerable profitable growth and the company's eventual dominance of a large sector of the market for watches.

THE MORE SIGNIFICANT MISMATCHES

As we have seen, possible mismatches may occur between:

1 the system of values and the real-life situation in the environment
2 the system of values and the organization
3 the organization and the environmental situation
4 different parts of the value system
5 different parts of the organization
6 the strategies adopted to deal with different parts of the environment.

Any review of a company and its relationship with its environment as a stage in a process of organizational change should, therefore, take all these possible sources of problems into account. The competence with which these analyses are carried out and the priorities which are set for dealing with the problems identified will be governing factors in the task of coping with environmental change. Another decisive factor will, of course, be the calibre of the company's resources for solving the problems identified, or maybe for preventing the mismatches from becoming significant in the first place, if this is possible.

Perhaps the more difficult and far reaching problems to resolve are those which result from mismatches involving the company's system of values. It is not easy to change ideas, beliefs or values which are firmly entrenched in an organization without radically changing the organization itself.

A catch here, of course, is that, with the wrong beliefs, it might not be possible to initiate the necessary changes in the organization. Nevertheless, perhaps the most essential steps for any organization in coping with the changing demands of its business environment, are to find some way of:

(a) formulating and keeping an up to date and realistic set of ideas, beliefs and values
(b) ensuring that the values are widely shared throughout the organization.

Once some way is found of doing this, the task of bringing the other important factors back into tune is then simplified.

INVOLVING ALL EMPLOYEES

It should be clear that the task of helping a company to adapt satisfactorily to its changing environment is one of keeping the company, its values, the strategies it is using and its situation in its environment in a state of congruence. At the same time it should be evident that this task requires resources greater than those of one small group acting in isolation, eg the corporate planners, MBO specialists, management development advisers, external consultants etc. The process of organizational change aimed at achieving this task must include some way of freeing people *throughout the organization* from entrenched ideas and beliefs which are no longer appropriate to the company's situation.

This can be facilitated by:

1 exposing more individuals, groups and 'task forces' to the changing demands of the external environment so that they are not wholly preoccupied with day to day operational activities
2 giving them the task of coping with the effects of changes in some part of the external environment – and initially helping them to acquire the expertise necessary to do this
3 encouraging them to learn from their experiences – helping them to modify their existing ideas, beliefs and values in the light of this new learning.

Unless these things are done there is little real chance that the fundamental shifts in policy and practice which may be seen to be required by the more far sighted individuals in the company will take place; the necessary changes will be frustrated by the people who must, in the end, bring them about.

Essentially, the key to simulating a natural change process is to set up a series of activities involving as many senior and middle managers as possible, for:

1 identifying and rectifying relevant mismatches
2 stimulating the individual and organizational learning which can trigger off the necessary changes within the organization
3 linking key members of the leading power group to the plans for change.

This in turn can lead to the creation of an effective system of 'participative management'.

3
Organizations can learn

The importance of individual and organizational learning to a natural change process cannot be overstressed. All organizations acquire knowledge, process it by organizing it into a 'system', and then sell the results to a customer. Think of your own company. Its founder had an idea for making money. He reckoned that this idea was saleable, and he was correct because the company survived. His idea was founded either on knowledge that he possessed or acquired personally, or knowledge which he knew he could 'buy' by employing the people who did possess it. However, as time passed the market for the product changed. If the company could not adapt by bringing new knowledge to bear on the original business idea then the company would have ceased to trade because not enough people would want its products. All innovation, research and development departments, and new product design are based on this simple truth.

All companies, if they are to survive, need to acquire new inputs of knowledge and to learn new forms of behaviour from time to time. If the company is one which deals with a well established product, in a stable market (eg a local bakery) the necessity to acquire new knowledge may be less urgent than if the company is dealing in products at the frontiers of technology (eg the computer industry). Here lies an obvious danger for 'stable' companies, in stable industries, with apparently stable markets. They may fail to recognize the need to innovate, to learn to adapt to changing situations, or if they recognize the need in theory, they may be unable to adapt their behaviour, (ie to learn). Learning has taken place only when there has been a change in behaviour. Think of some of Britain's basic industries: coal, steel, cotton, shipbuilding. Founded in the industrial revolution at the turn of the eighteenth century, they led the world. Although each one adapted to its changing environment in the late nineteenth and early twentieth centuries, they were unable to sustain a pace of change sufficient to maintain a lead in a rapidly changing world. Each industry either has gone through, or is in the process of going through, a traumatic period of change to try to make good previous tardiness in learning. There are many apparent reasons for this: poor management planning; lack of new products; poor design; restrictive working practices by trade unions and so on. We believe, however, that these are only symptomatic of the major cause of decline, namely, that the industries did not recognize the urgent need to learn to do new and/or different things. This chapter is about how organizations can improve their facility to learn.

WHAT IS ORGANIZATIONAL LEARNING?

The idea that an organization can learn is not an easy concept to grasp. On the one hand it is necessary to understand what it means for an organization to learn, on the other there is the need to clarify how the capacity of an organization to learn can be enhanced.

Organizational learning is not the same thing as individual learning, although obviously it depends on it. There are too many cases where an organization seems incapable of learning what every member of it already seems to know. Moreover, it is not enough that the chief executive should learn for the organization as a whole; there are many examples where it is evident that the man at the top has certain beliefs about how to proceed yet the organization goes its own way.

Although organizational learning is not merely individual learning, organizations can learn only through the experience and actions of the members who make up the organization.

It is useful to think of an organization as an agency for achieving certain specific objectives. In achieving these objectives it will perform a task or series of tasks. Organizational learning can be said to be taking place when the organization as a whole performs these individual tasks or collection of tasks more effectively as time goes on. The organization will have a collection of ideas and beliefs about how these tasks should be performed which will be modified in the light of the experience gained from carrying out the tasks. Although this collection of ideas can be regarded as an abstract thing, it nevertheless exists. It is this collection of ideas and beliefs which govern the actions of the organization and which organizational learning can modify.

A company's personnel management learned that employee turnover was reaching an unacceptable level and was beginning to threaten the performance of the company. Steps were taken to investigate the reason for the worker dissatisfaction, covering salary levels, fringe benefits and other factors which contribute to job satisfaction. The relevant factors were then modified leading to greater stability in the workforce.

This is a case of the relevant members of the company responding to changes in the internal and external environments by detecting mismatches which they could rectify and so maintain acceptable forms of organizational behaviour. In this example, the individuals concerned can be regarded as agents of organizational learning.

It might be that the personnel manager might be reluctant to approach the higher levels of management to modify the salary and other arrangements or that, if so approached, the latter would refuse to make the necessary changes. In this case individual learning can be said to have occurred, but organizational learning has not taken place. The individuals in this case have not functioned effectively as agents of organizational learning. Consequently, it should be clear from this illustration that no organizational learning can take place without individual learning, but individual learning, although necessary, is not a sufficient condition for organizational learning.

In this case, organizational learning would have occurred if salary scales, expense allowances or possibly job descriptions had been modified in accordance with the personnel manager's findings.

Every member of a company has his own mental picture of what the organization is, what it should be doing to be successful and what contribution he should be making to help in achieving this success. It is an integration of these mental pictures of the various members of the organization, which come together in collective interactions, which constitute the ideas which govern company behaviour.

The individuals' mental picture of the organization constantly changes as the company's situation changes. It would be easy for the pictures held by different individuals to be so diverse as to prevent any kind of organizational continuity occurring were it not for the fact that certain representations, or maps, of aspects of the organization hold them together. These representations, such as balance sheets, profit and loss statements, work flow diagrams, product/market matrices, statements of procedure, etc, are shared by individuals and guide their attempts to update their understanding of the changing organization. It is these mental pictures held by individuals, and partly shared with others, which provide the medium for organizational learning.

Organizations are continually engaged in transactions with their environments and as these environments change mismatches can arise between what the organization is doing and what it needs to do to carry out the transactions satisfactorily. Organizational learning can be said to have taken place when there is response to the mismatch, once identified, leading to subsequent changes in strategies and assumptions.

Thus organizational learning represents the sum of the learning of individuals and groups who work within the organization. People, and therefore organizations, learn best when they recognize a need to learn. A major task for senior managers is to help all who work in an organization to recognize the paramount importance of *their* need to learn if the organization is to survive.

The difference between learning and training

Because people learn most when they want to, and recognize a need for learning, it is important to distinguish between learning and training. Training is a systematic activity designed to enable an individual to acquire skill and knowledge. It is up to the individual to apply the result of the training in his work. This is when the learning takes place because there will have been a change in his behaviour, (ie in what he does). Not all learning requires training, but all training must be translated into learning if it is to be effective. Management is responsible for ensuring that training systems are adequate and that situations are created which will encourage appropriate learning to take place. Individuals must be responsible for their own learning and be willing to adapt to new developments. The successful organization is one where this fact is recognized.

Examples of organizational learning

The basic theory of learning curves is simple; the production worker learns as he works and the more often he repeats an operation the more efficient he becomes. This will result in a decline in the amount of direct labour required for each unit of production. This is a phenomenon that affects not only the individual worker but also groups of workers sharing a combined and complex task such as assembling an aeroplane.

During the Second World War the American aircraft industry recognized this fact and, moreover, determined that the rate of improvement in affecting this complex task was regular enough to be predictable. It was recognized that a learning pattern was occurring with considerable regularity. Furthermore, it was not long before various airframe companies had established certain standards of learning which were then used as a basis for predicting direct labour input.

The Stanford Research Institute was commissioned to carry out a statistical study covering the majority of aircraft produced during the Second World War. The result of this was the development of a series of learning curves which represented the average experience for various categories of aeroplanes – fighters, bombers and so forth. Although these curves were all different in terms of their starting points, (ie the labour input for the first plane of a particular type), the great majority had one characteristic in common, their rate of improvement. It was this fact essentially that started speculation about a general theory of learning curves.

The rate of improvement which was found to hold true for the operations covered by the survey was such that once production on a plane got going the fourth unit required about 80 per cent as much direct labour as the second, the tenth 80 per cent as much as the fifth, the two-hundredth 80 per cent as much as the hundredth, and so on, in each case a reduction of 20 per cent between doubled quantities. Because the rate of improvement seemed to compare so consistently they concluded that the aircraft industry's rate of learning was approximately 80 per cent between doubled quantities This fact is illustrated in the figure below.

Figure 2
Learning curve for the production of the B-29 plane

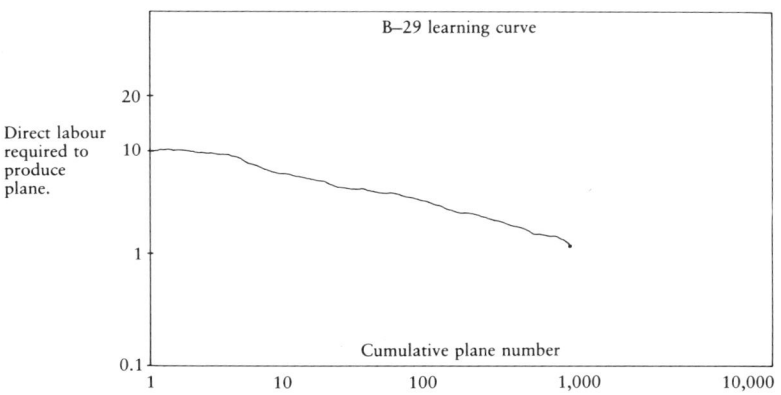

This standard is applied to this day in analysing a variety of procurement, production and costing problems within the industry and within particular companies.

The learning curve phenomenon was accounted for by a number of factors. The first was that learning in the literal sense took place amongst the workers and management in carrying out a complex task, (ie the production of an aeroplane). The second was that a whole series of other factors, amongst which management innovation could be regarded as the most significant, were also considered to be important. However, because of the consistant behaviour of the curve, learning, in a literal sense, continued to be the dominant influence. The belief that organizational learning was responsible for the improvement was also strengthened by the fact that the more the opportunities provided for learning, (ie the greater the number of aircraft produced), the greater the improvement.

The figure of 80 per cent learning between doubled quantities was achieved from the study of assembly work, since, in that type of work, there was a relatively large scope for learning. In machine work where the ability to reduce labour hours was greatly restricted by the fact that the machine could not learn to move any faster, the approximate rate of learning was found to be 90 per cent (ie a 10 per cent reduction in labour hours) for tasks which have actually three-quarter machine time and one-quarter assembly time, rather than the 80 per cent for assembly only.

These examples are useful indicators of the way in which organizations can learn to improve their performance in carrying out complex tasks. This is one form of learning which is essential if a company is to cope with a changing environment.

The more complex form of organizational learning

The examples described above have one thing in common. Learning is concerned primarily with effectiveness, or how best to achieve existing goals and objectives, and how best to get performance within limits or norms regarded as acceptable by the organization. There are occasions when a more complex form of learning is required and this is where correcting mismatches requires a learning cycle which also has to modify the existing values of norms of the organization in question.

This type of learning, and it is one of the main concerns in this book, is more difficult to achieve and can go wrong in many cases.

The manager of a hotel which was losing money implemented a number of recommendations for improving profitability made by the management of the group to which the hotel belonged. The recommendations mainly related to giving his managers (ie of catering, bars, conference facilities, etc) greater responsibility for the profitability of the operations they controlled and to setting up accounting and other systems to facilitate this change. The hotel was later studied by a team of managers from the same group, but responsible for other types of business than hotels. Their findings made it evident that there was still considerable scope for improvement in those things the hotel manager had already changed. Initially, this led to a conflict between the hotel manager and the members of the study group which was resolved in a series of discussions between the two sides which helped the manager to bring his own interpretation in line with that of the study group. He then modified the organization still further and within a short space of time the hotel became profitable.

This example illustrates that the changes initiated with an eye to effectiveness or improved efficiency under existing norms may be inadequate and unsatisfactory when compared with what is possible under another set of achievable norms, or values. An important feature of this example was that management left to themselves, and working within existing norms, arrived at conclusions that they should attempt to do better what they already knew how to do. The conclusions reached by the study group based on a higher level of performance achieved in another company, indicated that much more fundamental changes were necessary.

With this type of learning the detecting of mismatches ultimately leads not only to changes in strategies and assumptions for effective performance, but also to changes in the norms which define effective performance. It is the kind of learning to which the intervention of someone from outside the organization might be essential. The kind of situation from which this type of learning usually arises is through a conflict between the members or groups within the organization about the requirements for success. For example:

> The head of the subsidiary unit of a large computer firm believed that growth should be obtained organically by expanding the existing business in a natural way. His superior, however, held the view that adequate growth could be achieved only by acquiring other businesses, in addition to growth in the existing business. The conflict of views led to an impasse which was resolved only when the manager of the subsidiary concerned voluntarily engaged in a detailed learning process which embraced:
>
> (a) carrying out a detailed survey of the opportunities for growth open to the existing business which also highlighted the limited nature of those opportunities
> (b) gaining some familiarity with the process of company takeover, investigating some of the possible companies and gauging the effects that their takeover might have on more growth.
>
> This led to his acceptance of higher growth targets and of the need to takeover one or more other businesses if the planned growth was to be achieved.

The importance of this example is that it illustrates a conflict in which one side is basing its judgement on a firmly held belief or attitude acquired from experience gained up to that time, which was subsequently modified by testing this belief against the reality of the company's true situation. The fact that it was ultimately resolved and how this was done raises the question of 'how does one modify people's ideas, beliefs and attitudes?' without attempting to manipulate the people concerned. This is a critical question which managers must learn to understand if they wish to help their organizations to cope with the changing environment.

CHANGING IDEAS, BELIEFS AND VALUES

A person's ideas, beliefs and values, or attitudes, tend to constrict, conserve and stabilize his world. It is for this reason that a person's response to a problem in a working situation can often be predicted. However, as the world in which he is living changes, different types of behaviour might be required to cope with the newer problems presented even though the setting or surroundings in which these changes occur might remain the same. The required changes in behaviour will be facilitated if there are appropriate changes in the ideas, beliefs and values of the person concerned.

The problem of changing values and attitudes and, at the same time avoiding attempts to manipulate people, is perhaps the most urgent psychological problem of today. It bedevils many aspects of industrial and company life and is a problem which managements must tackle if they hope to succeed.

People working together in groups also develop group ideas, beliefs, values and norms as they attempt to cope with their common problems. Just as in the case of an individual, certain of the solutions which are attempted become firmly established and are transmitted to successive members of the group as part of the 'culture' of the group. This also applies to larger group formations such as organizations, communities and societies. Again, as with individuals, the need to change the behaviour of groups within a company is of paramount importance if the company is to cope with the changing environment (eg as with the 'quality circle' concept).

Research has shown that a number of factors can exert an appreciable influence on the behaviour of groups and individuals within an organization. Leadership, the extent to which ideas and beliefs are shared with others, the kind of people in one's working group and the extent to which they are forced to act in certain ways can all influence individual behaviour. The information to which people are exposed, particularly when it comes from an unimpeachable source, can also be important.

One of the most effective ways of changing ideas, beliefs, values and attitudes, and ultimately behaviour, and one which is fundamental to the approach to change advocated in this book, is to use group problem solving. A judicious choice of the problems, and of the membership of the problem solving groups, can have a powerful influence on the acquisition of new forms of behaviour. This is particularly the case where the choice of the problems for investigation has the backing of top management and demands that new knowledge should be acquired for confronting existing ideas and beliefs.

Encouraging experimentation

What needs to be done to be successful is constantly changing as the environment changes. Management must appreciate that most of what has been accepted as 'true' at one time or another has at some later stage turned out not to be the case. This proposition is as valid in the world of business as it is in the worlds of science or philosophy. Yet the tendency is for people to constantly reinterpret the evidence they obtain from their business transactions in order to maintain their existing beliefs. There is a reluctance to admit that they are wrong, particularly in a culture where to be wrong is to be punished.

It is not only pride in our existing knowledge or a fear of punishment, however, that makes us cling to our out of date beliefs or theories. This tendency can often stem either from ignorance of what is happening in the world outside the company or from a lack of confidence in one's ability to analyse and to interpret properly data which does not fit into our existing scheme of things. This latter effect is particularly likely when this kind of data is arriving 'thick and fast' from many directions. Perhaps it is not surprising that, as the environment becomes more uncertain, people should tend to hold on to strategies and methods of working which have stood them in good stead in the past. Yet, somehow, a way must be found to discourage these tendencies.

This is not to say that we should abandon our beliefs and theories lightly because this would lead us to an uncritical attitude towards the tests we apply. This, in turn, would mean that the theories themselves were not tested as thoroughly as they should be. What it does mean for top management is that they should endeavour to create a climate in their companies which encourages people to adopt a more experimental approach to business. This implies finding ways of helping their staff to recognize that developing a new business, or modifying an established business to cope with changing circumstances, relies on using a variety of approaches. These include problem solving, trial and error, learning new things, modifying existing beliefs about what is needed for success and, in particular, a high degree of mutual trust between the participants in the enterprise.

All levels of management must realize that in dealing with a rapidly changing environment mistakes are inevitable. What is important is that when taking a step into new and unexplored territory, it should be taken on the basis of 'the best of our knowledge' at the time. We should not, however, automatically expect it to be the best possible step otherwise we shall be tempted to defend it unreasonably, even if it does not achieve the results we had hoped for. Rather, it should be seen as the first step in a learning process which may lead to a number of changes in direction before the required goal is reached.

Viewed in this way, the task of developing a business is seen to be an experimental one. In consequence, success or failure is largely governed by the company's capability of learning from the experiences it meets. It is important to emphasize the need to learn to all concerned. Moreover, it is the task of top management to provide whatever support and assistance people may need in engaging in the 'uncertain' process of learning – uncertain because it is all too common in business for an individual or a group of people to fail to learn from their experiences.

4
How to manage a company's learning

It is clear that the process of adapting to dramatically changing circumstances, particularly where the necessary process of change has to be consciously managed, requires a company to engage in an extensive programme of learning. Many individuals will have to learn to do new things, as must the organization as a whole or in part.

The new knowledge and skills which have to be acquired will depend on the kind of problems which the company has to solve and will differ appreciably from one enterprise to another. It will also differ depending on the parts of the organization in which a change of behaviour is required. What is important is that no company today can afford to allow the necessary learning to occur haphazardly. It must happen as a result of a managed process.

It is worth pointing out here what every good teacher knows, namely that you cannot teach anyone anything. All that can be done is to stimulate concern for a particular topic and allow people to acquire the necessary information in an orderly and interesting manner. If people see no point in learning or if they can't relate the new information to their existing knowledge and ideas, they 'switch off', unless something is done to prevent this happening. It is part of the task of managing company learning to ensure that this does not happen and that, where a conflict does arise between the existing ideas and beliefs of some part of the organization and the newer information coming in, the latter is considered on its merits and is not rationalized out of existence.

Recognizing the need to learn

Conducting a programme of learning for an organization as a whole or for part of it is not an easy task. It will only take place effectively if there is sufficient concern in the organization that there is something wrong which can be put right, or there is scope for improving things. Moreover, there must be a sufficient awareness that whatever is wrong is likely to have a severe effect on the company's performance, possibly to the extent of threatening the well-being of the organization as a whole or some important part of it.

In an organization which has a forceful leader or alternatively an autocratic system of management then it may only be necessary to convince the man at the top that some internal changes are necessary if the company is to continue to cope with the environment it is attempting to exploit.

In the case of a big, complex, successful, organization where charisma and autocracy are suspect, the situation may be different. In such a company power is usually spread throughout the organization in a way which prevents any one individual taking the kind of action which might threaten other people's identity or vested interests. In this case the development of concern and the recognition that the company needs to learn about new things is still essential but is more difficult to generate. This concern or appreciation of the need to learn must be shared by a sufficiently large number of people in positions of power before effective change can be initiated.

In the first place it might be that only one or two individuals in a company sense that something is wrong and are prepared to draw the attention of their colleagues to the mismatches which are developing. It might be that these people have little impact initially or may even be rejected as being out of tune with the organization's needs. Yet, somehow, this concern or appreciation of the need of the organization to learn new things must be spread throughout enough of the key people in the organization to ensure that some form of study can be undertaken to assess the extent of the problem.

A PROGRAMME FOR MANAGING THE COMPANY'S LEARNING

Once sufficient concern has been developed and an interest in learning has been generated, the management of a company's learning will generally involve the following steps:

1 establishing what needs to be learned and who should learn it
2 identifying or creating situations from which the necessary learning can be derived
3 assessing what has been learned and identifying further learning needs.

These steps are described more fully below.

1 Establishing what needs to be learned and who should learn it

The decisions about the problem areas to be studied and who should be involved in the necessary investigations are critical in managing a company's learning. It means identifying areas in the company where some or all of the following conditions apply:

(a) there is a need to do something different from what is being done at present, but with the possibility that no one is entirely clear about what this is or how it should be done
(b) there is a need to continue doing what is done now but to do it better
(c) there is no awareness of the need to do things differently yet the need does exist.

It might be that some of the problem areas are obvious to a careful observer, others might require an intensive search before they are recognized. On the other hand, a wide ranging discussion between the senior managers in the firm on the issues which need to be resolved if the firm is to achieve adequate levels of performance in, say, five years time is an effective way of identifying areas requiring more detailed study. This can often lead to the company's senior managers agreeing on the problems to be studied, on what should be the priorities and on who should be involved in the investigations. This in turn increases the likelihood that the studies will trigger off any necessary organizational change.

In deciding who in a company should be involved in the learning process one should remember that two of the main aims of the process are:

(a) to modify the ideas, beliefs and values of key people, and
(b) to generate changes in the company's behaviour in its response to the environment.

Consequently, it is desirable to involve the key people in some way in those power groups in the company which can exert the necessary influence on both the decision making and on the implementation of the changes of strategy or practice which might be decided on.

2 Identifying or creating situations from which the necessary learning can be derived

Learning in a company occurs as a result of a complex cycle of detecting errors and correcting them. The cycle begins when people acting on the basis of their existing ideas and beliefs detect a mismatch between what they expect to happen as a result of their actions and what actually occurs. This process raises questions about those ideas and beliefs. The next step in the cycle is the process of correcting the mismatch. Organizational learning will have occurred when organizational ideas, beliefs and practices have been modified in order to eliminate the mismatch, otherwise the individuals may have learned but not the organization.

The various steps which, if carried out properly, can form the cycle of both organizational and individual learning in a

particular set of circumstances, (ie leading to subsequent changes in behaviour), are as follows:
(a) establish the present situation and how it is changing by a fact finding exercise
(b) clarify what is to be achieved (ie the goals)
(c) identify the obstacles or mismatches and their causes which might prevent the achievement of those goals
(d) develop a plan of action for both correcting the mismatches and achieving the goals
(e) take action
(f) evaluate and generalize the results of action.

At which point the cycle begins again.
These steps in greater detail are as follows.

Establish the present situation

This involves carrying out a comprehensive fact finding exercise covering all aspects of that part of the organization where the present activities do not meet the objectives presently considered desirable. The danger here is that the investigation will be superficial and will not provide a true picture of the situation. Critical aspects of this stage are the boundaries set for the study, how the study is structured, where it begins, where it goes and who does it. An important feature will be the information needed for a detailed understanding of the situation. The information, which is in theory available, may not be obtainable without considerable effort and the passage of time. It might be that the methods for collecting the information are inadequate or make an effective analysis of the facts impossible. In this case it is necessary to proceed on a 'best guess' basis, which can be refined in due course.

Clarify what is to be achieved

This is the stage in which an attempt is made to establish where the organization wishes to be at some time in the future. The target here will usually be some desired form of organizational behaviour which is different from that which prevails at the present time. It might be a reduction in staff turnover or an increased competitiveness in the activities of the company's buyers. Whatever is the case, it is important to have some target at which to aim even though it might be a rapidly moving one. Having as clear an idea as possible of where one wishes to be at some time in the future makes it easier to identify the mismatches which must be corrected and the problems which must be solved if an acceptable future is to be assured.

Identify mismatches and their causes

This stage in which significant mismatches are identified and their causes determined is achieved by reviewing and analysing the information obtained in the fact finding exercise in the light of the objectives of the exercise. It can go wrong for a number of reasons. Mismatches may not be identified if the original fact finding exercise was inadequate. It might be difficult to identify the source or cause of the mismatches, particularly where this would mean questioning existing norms or cherished organizational beliefs held by the people conducting the study. Again, the methods used to analyse the information might be totally inadequate, or perhaps the objectives to be achieved are not properly defined or understood. These possibilities, which can lead to an ineffective identification of the key problems which must be solved if real progress is to be made, should be taken into account when designing the initial fact finding exercise and also at a later stage by any change agents who may be assisting with the process.

Develop a plan of action

This is the stage at which effective or competent solutions will be developed to correct the mismatches and their causes identified in the earlier stage. Its effectiveness will depend on the clarity with which the objectives and problems have been defined and on the calibre of the problem solving resources available to the organization. Many organizations do not have the talents necessary to produce good quality solutions to the problems identified. Too often a discussion about solutions loses its way in negative thinking:

    We can't do that because ....

    We've tried it before ....

    We need others' agreement and we'll never get it ....

Again, if any new strategies devised are to be implemented properly it is important that the people who will be responsible for doing this should have been involved in defining the problem to the extent that they are prepared to accept ownership of it and its solution.

Take action

It is surprising how often taking a new course of action or making a change in existing practices can run into difficulties. Often this will stem from the fact that the programmes for change have been formulated by those who will be least affected by the changes when they take place. This type of event frequently occurs on the shop floor when a work study engineer has been requested to draw up plans for the reorganization of a production unit. No doubt he has discussed what was required with the foreman and he will have studied the work patterns of the operators. However, unless he has developed his thinking and his proposals with the operators, the plans finally produced are likely to meet resistance. The reason is clear: we all detest change when it is sprung upon us.

At the management level this point needs to be understood. Frequently, top management decisions and plans for change are frustrated by the levels below because the latter have not been involved in the learning process which has identified the need for the change. An alternative approach is to involve those affected by change in the formulation of programmes of action. It implies giving teams of managers responsibility for ensuring that the business, or aspects of it, remain congruent with the environment in which it operates.

It also involves taking a risk because the action may not be successful. Success is likely to depend on the work of people other than the person who initiates the action, and who has the ultimate responsibility for its success. This means that the more everyone concerned with the action is committed to its success, the greater the chances will be that the action will achieve the objectives hoped for. There is thus an important link between organizational learning and individual commitment to change.

Evaluate and generalize the results of the action

People learn by taking action and having knowledge of the results of that action to compare with what they expected to happen, ie by measuring their performance against suitable standards. The less time that elapses between taking action and knowing whether the action has achieved what was intended, the more learning will take place. That is why capital investment decisions are so difficult to take. There is normally a long time gap between taking the investment decision and being able to evaluate its results. By the time results are available conditions may have changed and it is difficult to learn the lessons which will ensure that future investment decisions are influenced correctly by the experience of previous occasions.

3 Assessing what has been learned and determining further learning needs

It is important to assess the progress of the planned learning tasks in the company and if possible evaluate any improvements in performance which might result from them. If this can be done, it will often help reinforce the lessons which have been learned and will help to prevent the changed behaviour reverting to the earlier mode.

Various methods can be used to assess the effectiveness and progress of the learning process. For the board of directors of a company faced with the need to learn to cope more with strategic issues rather than procedural ones, the change in the contents of the minutes of their meetings, the topics discussed and the decisions made provided a useful way of measuring progress. The progress of the learning of a team of potential general managers asked to study the business of a subsidiary company engaged in transporting containers across the Irish

Sea was measurable by the worthwhile ideas they produced which they successfully persuaded the management of the company to adopt.

It is important to choose an appropriate method for assessing progress at an early stage in the process as it can be a useful discipline which may have a considerable impact on the kind of tasks selected to facilitate learning. It is easy, of course, to say that it is not possible to assess the results of the efforts being made to improve the performance of the organization. The fact that many extraneous events can have an effect on company performance which override the intentions and actions of its managers is a possibility to which adequate consideration must be given. Yet it is wrong to overestimate the effects of these events and to accept that for this reason it is impossible to assess the effect of managerial or perhaps supporting staff initiatives on organizational performance. The truth of the matter is, provided that those managing and their supporting staff focus their attention on the *key issues* affecting company performance rather than those peripheral ones which may or may not be significant, then the ability to measure the real performance of management (and the effectiveness of its advisers) should become more of a practical reality.

If learning is to proceed satisfactorily it may be necessary to provide resources to assist the managers involved in the process. These may be change agents of various kinds, specialists in solving various forms of problem or educationalists whose task could be to make available to the participants a knowledge of the techniques for fact finding, analysis or problem solving. The important requirement here, however, would be to ensure that the company's own managers firmly retain the responsibility for the analysis and problem solving using the specialists as additional resources to be managed.

The learning process can go wrong in many ways and for many reasons. The fact finding might be inadequate because slip shod methods have been used. The mismatches and problems identified might miss the really significant ones because certain norms or values were not questioned. The solutions to the problems identified and the plans formulated to put these solutions into practice might be inadequate because of a deficiency in the company's problem solving capability. The solutions, even though sound and appropriate, might not be implemented satisfactorily, if at all, if the people concerned in making them work were not party to developing the solutions.

It is evident, therefore, that if the inquiry into deficiencies in an existing organization is to be conducted properly, it must be managed carefully. Moreover, it must be managed by someone who is prepared to question the existing values of the organization and who is part of, or at least has the support of, the key power group of the organization.

What needs to be learned

It has already been mentioned that the new knowledge and skills which a company needs to acquire in order to adapt to a changed environment depends on the kind of problems it has to solve. Moreover, the learning required will differ appreciably from one enterprise to another. Chapter 9 describes in considerable depth the kind of learning which one particular company had to acquire and details of the steps which were taken in order to facilitate the learning. The set of questions given in the appendix on page 135 were used to guide this learning process. They can be applied equally well to most, if not all, business organizations.

It is sufficient here to give some examples of the kinds of knowledge and skills which had to be acquired by individuals and groups in various companies faced with the task of coping with business environments which were new to them. In most cases this learning was essential before the companies could begin to make progress. Brief details are also given of the kind of situations which were devised to help the learning take place.

Companies as a whole had to learn:

(a) that the ideas on which their business was built and had achieved success were no longer valid
(b) that their dealings with customers, etc were no longer

satisfactory (eg perhaps in terms of products, acceptability, pricing, deliveries, quality of service provided, etc) because competition had increased dramatically as a result of excess capacity in the industry.

This kind of learning required a comparison of the company's actions and performance with those of significant competitors or perhaps the industry as a whole. It also needed a detailed fact finding exercise to identify significant mismatches between what happens and what should happen, particularly with regard to the company's product range and methods of trading and their acceptability to existing and potential customers.

A board of directors had to learn:

(a) that the real nature of their company was appreciably different from what was considered to be the case, ie that it was a collection of different but interlinked businesses rather than a single business and that each of these sub-businesses required different strategies to be successful
(b) to direct what was now seen as a portfolio of businesses each making different demands on the company's resources and each offering different kinds of return at varying degrees of risk
(c) to focus their attention more on strategic issues rather than operational ones.

In this particular case the necessary learning was stimulated and guided at a series of two day meetings away from the office. At each meeting new management concepts were introduced prior to sessions relating them both to the company's strategic position and to the key problems affecting the company as a whole which needed to be treated as priorities.

A chief executive had to learn:

(a) that his role was not to be the main driving force behind a single business but to be a 'diplomat' encouraging subordinates to drive different parts of the business portfolio

(b) how to handle this new role.

This learning occurred over a lengthy period of time during which the organization of the company concerned gradually changed from a functional to a matrix structure in line with the approach described in this book. In the case discussed here the external change agent was largely responsible for helping the chief executive to appreciate both the newer requirements of his changing organization and the implications of these in relation to his future role.

Individual executive directors and departmental heads had to learn:

> that although they had their own ideas of responsibility and clear-cut departmental performance targets to meet, it was the contribution which they made to the total business or businesses as a whole which in the long run had over-riding importance.

Staff specialists such as management accountants and computer specialists had to learn:

> that the information they should produce was that which was found to be needed to run the business and was different from what they initially thought was necessary.

Managers at all levels had to learn:

(a) to modify their styles of management to accommodate the wider distribution of responsibilities for running parts of the business which has often been required as part of the change process
(b) to modify their behaviour towards their subordinates in order to stimulate creativity in solving some of the newer problems which were encountered.

> The learning in all these instances resulted from the needs of the individuals concerned to keep abreast of the programmes of change being implemented in their companies. In most cases the necessary changes in outlook, understanding and behaviour were facilitated by the external and internal change agents.
> Operators often had to acquire new basic skills in

order to produce the new products or services on which their company's survival depended. For example, many temporary secretaries who were able to get by if they could use a typewriter needed to learn to use different types of word processors, each of which have distinct features. These skills were acquired from a programme of tuition specifically designed to meet the needs of the employment agency which provided the temporary secretarial service.

In many of the case examples above the necessary learning has not been achieved easily. Often it has only occurred when people have been convinced from their own experience of the situations that their original beliefs, opinions or behaviour were no longer appropriate.

USING EDUCATIONAL ASSISTANCE

A number of industrialists have called on the assistance of educationalists from external sources to help them progress their companies' learning. The examples below illustrate some of the methods which the staff of the Management and Business Development Unit of Kingston Regional Management Centre have developed to assist key individuals or teams of managers to learn how to make a more effective contribution to the performance of their companies.

The type of problems which have been addressed have occurred at all levels in organizations. They have concerned the development of whole businesses, carrying out of major projects and also helping individual managers to cope more effectively with their jobs. Examples of the type of problems the unit has considered are as follows:

(a) Working with a team of senior managers to review the nature of a transport *business* in order to understand its problems of growth and development and then to develop plans for improving its profitability and general effectiveness.

(b) Working with a *project* team to consider how public catering services at a number of sites could be carried out more cost effectively.

(c) Helping the *head of a business* providing data processing services to develop a better understanding of his business in strategic and organizational terms, the aim being to develop a more effective approach to running the business.
(d) Working with a scientist who had been promoted to be the *manager* of a new product development team, the aim being to help him to cope more effectively with his job and to improve his working relationship with his boss.

The role of the staff of the unit in these activities has been that of management educator rather than that of a conventional management consultant. This difference between education and consultancy is more than an academic distinction. The role in the main has been to act as a resource to the managers concerned by providing them with a knowledge of and guidance in the use of appropriate techniques and methods for fact finding, analysis, interpretation, planning and problem solving.

A particularly useful aspect of this way of working has been that since the problems were solved by the managers themselves, the solutions were more rapidly implemented than would have been the case if the solutions had been imposed on them by top management acting solely on advice from a consultant, for example.

WHO SHOULD MANAGE A COMPANY'S LEARNING?

It is not enough that a company's learning should be well designed, planned and executed, it is also important that the process is an explicit one. In other words, the stage should be reached where learning is recognized by all employees as a key element of the process by which the company keeps itself abreast of changing events in the outside world. In fact, a company or any organization must acquire the ability to manage its own learning.

It must be clear that this is not solely the job of the

company's training manager. The activities which are required are of the kind that call for direct involvement or at least the support of the chief executive since they can consume a considerable amount of the time and effort of the company's top and senior managers. It may require frequent meetings between executives where time is specifically devoted to learning more about the environment, the organization itself and the relationship between the two.

The programme of learning needed by a company to help it to achieve a state of congruence with its environment will in all probability consist of a number of closely linked yet distinct problem-solving projects. These must be part of a dynamic process to take account of the fact that the company's problems are changing and in a state of flux. For this reason it is important that the programme as a whole and the individual projects within it must be managed by people who have the power and authority to make necessary changes from time to time to the terms of reference, the resourcing or the priorities given to the various parts of the programme.

If possible one individual should be given overriding responsibility for managing the company's learning and he/she must have the ear of top management. He must also have considerable intellectual capacity, a sensitivity to the learning needs of the company as a whole and of key individuals and the ability to initiate and conduct participative learning tasks which will satisfy these needs. Experience so far suggests that the person responsible for corporate planning, if one exists, can be suited to this type of role provided that he has a sound conceptual grasp of strategic planning, is not too firmly wedded to any particular set of techniques and has an appreciation of the importance of learning as a means of effecting organizational change. The person responsible for management training and development might also be suited for this task. More important than the job title of the person concerned is his personal competence and position of real influence in the organization.

5
Strategic planning as a process of learning and change

The learning and change process required by a company which finds itself no longer in touch with its present day environment needs to be fundamental. It must also be comprehensive, taking in all the major parts of the organization. Thus strategic planning which incorporates detailed appraisals of both a company's present situation and its current environment can provide the main vehicle for both organizations and individuals to learn to adjust to and to cope with a changing business environment. Figure 3 below shows how the environment, the company and its goals and objectives need to interrelate. One cannot be separated from the other in a successful and well integrated company.

What we have identified as strategic planning is, therefore, that collection of activities which aims to establish and maintain harmony between:

(a) important needs in the business environment which the company is seeking to satisfy, ie the needs of customers, suppliers, sources of finance, expectations of the labour market, etc
(b) what the company is doing in relation to relevant individuals or organizations in the environment to satisfy

Figure 3

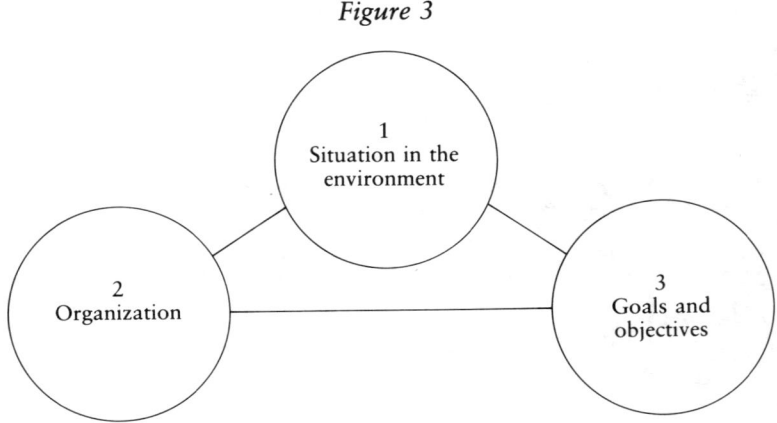

these needs in such a way that the objectives and goals of the enterprise are also met, in particular the business or businesses from which the company is making its money
(c) the organization itself, ie its systems such as marketing, manufacturing, procurement, rewards and punishments and management controls, etc
(d) the goals and objectives of the enterprise.

In order to be effective this process should be conducted in a number of well defined stages which are consistent with the steps in the cycle of organizational learning outlined in Chapter 4. These are detailed below in the following eight stages.

STAGE I: ESTABLISHING THE COMPANY'S PRESENT SITUATION

1 Collecting relevant facts about the company's present situation and how this appears to be changing. This should include a study of:

(a) the needs of its present business environment or at least that part of it which is relevant, or likely to be relevant, and also how these needs are changing. This applies particularly to the company's market place and possible sources of essential supplies

(b) the businesses in which the company is engaged and how they satisify external needs, taking competitors into account

(c) the key parts of the organization which are being used to support the company's businesses and how well they are doing this.

The answers to the questions given in the appendix on page 135 will provide the necessary facts.

2 Analysing and evaluating the information obtained from this fact finding study in order to identify any important mismatches between the above factors which detract from short and longer term performance. This analysis should identify the strengths, weaknesses, opportunities and threats which are likely to affect the company. It should also begin to identify the company's 'business idea(s)', or, in other words, the company's particular way(s) of making money, and any specific advantages the company may have over its competitors.

It is important in the analysis to appreciate that the success of a business depends ultimately on the extent to which it makes a crucial or strategic contribution to the larger system of which the business forms part. For example, the De Beers Corporation which is one of the world's major suppliers of diamonds is a crucial contributor to the jewellery industry. Again a prominent reinsurance company in the City of London is successful because it provides the essential service of spreading the risks and liabilities of major insurance transactions between a number of insurance companies.

It should also be appreciated that over the course of time the nature of a company's business can change significantly as a result of growth in different directions. During this time the management team can be so preoccupied with supporting the growth that it is unable to maintain an objective view of what is happening to the company. This state of affairs more often prevails with a company which is successful, perhaps beyond its original expectations.

The textile company referred to in Chapter 8 had in the few years prior to the study been extremely successful, had increased its product range considerably and had penetrated many new markets. The management team still retained the impression that the company's business was the relatively simple one of providing fabrics for a limited variety of end uses. Once the company's situation was studied in depth it soon became apparent that the company was engaged in a number of quite separate businesses each one of which required different treatment if the best results were to be obtained.

STAGE II: DETERMINING WHERE WE WANT TO BE

A review should be made of the objectives and goals the company is attempting to achieve to assess their reasonableness in the light of the analyses described above. They may need to be modified to take account of the difficulties likely to be experienced in correcting any mismatches which are detracting from performance.

Where the business environment is highly unstable, progress can be made only one step at a time. After each step the position must be reviewed again before the next course of action can be determined. This, in effect, represents a true learning process which is a characteristic of a developing business breaking new ground or attempting to cope with rapidly changing circumstances.

STAGE III: DIAGNOSIS

It is important to identify the problems to be solved, the barriers to profitable growth to be overcome and the mismatches to be rectified in order to achieve the desired vision or goals.

> The Timex Watch Company achieved a large share of the watch market once it had overcome its problem of distribution, ie by selling through retail outlets such as

drugstores and supermarkets. However, further growth was inhibited by the fact that people were accustomed to owning only one watch. By convincing people that watches were fashion items which should match the kind of clothing being worn, people were persuaded to own a number of watches.

STAGE IV: PREPARING PLANS FOR ACHIEVING THE GOALS

Plans should be developed for overcoming the problems, barriers to growth and the mismatches identified. The planning should take account of any priorities which need to be observed. This is detailed planning which sets specific tasks, targets and schedules for individuals to achieve.

STAGE V: MODIFYING THE ORGANIZATION

During the course of assessing the company's present situation and developing plans for future action, it will be found that changes are necessary to the existing organization structure, to the resources available or to the methods and practices in current use. During this stage of the exercise the necessary changes will be determined and agreed. But organizational modification should arise from defined needs and not, as so often happens, take place before new goals have been agreed. Too often organizational change is used as a substitute for thinking about the fundamental causes of the problems which the organizational change is designed to overcome.

The stages described above are conventional steps in a strategic planning system with the possible exception of the emphasis that is placed on achieving congruence between the company and the needs of the larger system it is attempting to service. However, we are concerned with strategic planning as the main vehicle for both organizational and individual learning. There are three additional stages to be completed to enable learning to take place, shown as stages VI, VII and VIII below.

STAGE VI: IMPLEMENTING THE PLANS

During this stage any organizational changes decided upon should be made. Responsibility for implementing the plans should be allocated and the appointed personnel should be instructed to develop their own action plans for implementation against an agreed budget.

STAGE VII: MODIFYING INFORMATION AND CONTROL SYSTEMS

It is often found in carrying out this kind of exercise that the existing information and control systems can inhibit the initial fact finding and the preparation of plans since they were designed to accommodate the company's past situation rather than the present one. Consequently there is a paucity of the information required to understand the company's present situation. There might be insufficient data about markets and market trends, and financial or cost information systems might not be sufficiently well developed to indicate how the company makes its money or loses it.

If the plans which have been developed involve any significant changes in direction, (which is usually the case), then the existing systems will neither provide the information needed to measure progress nor enable corrective action to be taken. More particularly, the feedback needed for learning from the results of the actions taken will not be available.

An important stage, therefore, should be to modify the company's information and control systems to conform to the needs of the new organization which has been established. Management accounting information, marketing data, indicators of potential growth and actual performance in different product/market sectors and measures of the effectiveness of resource utilization are particularly important.

Stage VIII: Feedback, Review and Learning

In many ways this is the most important part of the process in that it entails observing and evaluating the results of the plans which have been implemented and using the assessment to modify some or all of the following:

(a) the vision or goals which are being sought
(b) the actions being taken
(c) the ideas and knowledge on which the original plans were based.

It is important that this review should be made with emphasis on what can be done to improve the situation further, rather than on defending past actions. It is perhaps useful to mention again that in a rapidly changing business world the successful development of a business is achieved by a process of experiment or trial and error and by learning from these experiences. Providing it can be viewed objectively, a mistake can often be as useful as a success provided individuals and the company are prepared to face up to and learn from it. It is, however, unfortunate that in many organizations anyone making a mistake is often punished severely, which, in the long run, leads to an organization which fails to learn because it employees are loathe to take risks and hence allows itself to get further and further out of touch with its real environment.

An important question to consider is that of the frequency with which reviews should be made and this may not be an easy question to answer.

In a company which had introduced a formal planning system involving the annual preparation of a three year forward plan, there was a tendency to review the results of the plan annually despite the fact that many of the individual action plans contained in the corporate plan required more frequent attention of top management. Consequently, whereas on one hand many plans failed because of the lack of amendment at the appropriate time, on the other some managers took action as they thought fit with the projects for which they were responsible and took no account of how their actions might affect the rest of the corporate plan. This ultimately led to the corporate planning activity falling into disrepute.

Although it is not possible to give a specific answer to the question 'how often should plans be reviewed?' it is useful to view the corporate plan as a collection of separate plans for action, each one of which has its own time cycle. Some plans need to be reviewed daily, others at less frequent intervals. It is best left to the people responsible for implementing the plans to decide at what intervals a review is needed although it is useful to assess the progress of all the individual plans before preparing the next formal annual plan and preferably at more frequent intervals, say quarterly.

A practical example of the way in which the strategic planning process has been used as a vehicle for organizational learning and the means by which a company has learned to cope with its changed business environment is given in Chapter 8.

ORGANIZING THE PLANNING AND IMPLEMENTATION

In generalizing about how planning should be organized, it is worth recapitulating on what we are trying to do to generate the right kind of learning and subsequent change. The people engaged in planning are being expected to:

1 learn to understand a business: what it is and how it has reached its present stage of development
2 develop an understanding of:
   (a) what is required for a successful business in the industry concerned
   (b) what is needed for the particular business under consideration
3 identify what needs are being satisfied by the business and how well this is being done particularly in comparison with competitors

4 question if the needs can be satisfied more effectively and if so, how
5 develop or agree to a vision of, or a set of goals for, the future
6 identify the problems or barriers in the way of achieving the 'vision' or goals
7 develop and implement plans for surmounting the obstruction to achieving the vision/goals. This may be a question merely of determining what the next step should be and then taking it
8 learn from the results of taking the 'next step' to ensure that subsequent steps will be better directed.

To start it is necessary to select one or more 'whole' businesses which can be studied and further developed. By 'whole' business is meant some area of business activity within the company which can be regarded as discrete, for example, a particular product/market sector.

The next step is to appoint groups consisting of, say, four or five executives to investigate them. The members of each group should preferably be chosen to represent each of the main functional disciplines such as production, marketing, finance and product development. This ensures that each group has available to it the various types of expertise necessary to understand the different aspects of the business. Having to carry out a study of a 'whole' business in one of the multi-discipline teams is a good way of helping specialists to understand how a 'whole' business functions. In addition, it also enables them to develop a better idea of the contribution which they can make to developing a business.

For the fact finding needed to determine the present situation in a business there is something to be gained by involving people who are not normally concerned with the business in question. They can view it in a more objective way than someone who is too closely engaged in the details of it. In the preparation of plans and the implementing stages, however, it is more desirable to involve people who already have a real commitment to the business concerned. Preference should also be given to people who have already shown that they possess entrepreneurial skills.

6
Barriers and aids to success

A number of important factors can aid or inhibit the use of the strategic planning process as the basis for the kind of organizational and individual learning which can help a company to become more effective in coping with its changing environment. Some of them are of a general nature, others assume significance at different stages in a company's development. This chapter considers some of the more important of these factors.

THE IMPORTANCE OF A VISION

A complaint which is levelled by many managers against the conventional corporate planning process is that it is unrealistic to attempt to define precisely where the organization expects to be or what it will be doing in, say, five years' time. The fact is that a manager's plans for tomorrow, let alone for five years' time, are often not achieved owing to unforeseen circumstances. One consequence is that many managers do not take corporate or business planning seriously.

Although this complaint may result from a lack of understanding of what corporate planning really is, it more often stems from the planners' attempts to be too positive and precise in making forecasts of the future, and in proposing long-term objectives. The business environment is changing rapidly, often in unpredictable ways. It is, therefore, unrealistic to attempt to be over-precise in making forecasts.

In the case of a mature business operating in a reasonably stable environment where technological innovation is a rare occurrence, the more conventional approach to corporate planning can be acceptable. Profit and growth objectives are set for, say, five years hence, projections are made of what can be expected from existing activities and plans are then prepared for what is thought to be necessary to ensure that the set objectives are met over the planning time cycle.

In the case of a business in an early stage of growth or of one which for a variety of reasons has failed significantly to keep step with the changing needs of its customers, suppliers or financiers and is consequently declining, this type of long-term planning is inappropriate. It might not be possible to describe either a likely end point at some time in the future or the way in which it can be reached. Yet for businesses of these kinds some indication of the desirable future attainments is required as a means of guiding future actions.

Some writers have used the term 'vision' to describe the flexible target which can be used for this purpose. It is not sufficiently concrete to be a goal. It should embrace the whole business or potential business. It should contain ideas about the market which is eventually to be dominated, the type of products or services to be offered to the market and the kind of organization and resources needed to make dominance possible. The 'vision' should be seen as a tool in the process of learning needed to develop a new business successfully or to reconstitute an older business which no longer meets the needs of today. The vision itself is modified as learning proceeds; consequently it not only guides the learning process but also acts as a measure of the effectiveness of the learning. As the learning proceeds the 'vision' becomes more specific and firmer goals can be established. An important consideration is that a 'vision' is meaningless unless it leads to a positive and immediate action geared to its realization. It is also important that the vision and the steps taken must be related both to the company's real situation and to its competence.

Perhaps the most important role a corporate planner can

play in a company which is faced with a rapidly changing business environment is to present top management continually with the scenarios and information needed to help them to acquire and maintain a 'vision' of the future which is sufficiently in tune with reality to provide adequate guidelines for directing the company affairs.

THE PROBLEM SOLVING CAPABILITY

It is not enough merely to identify mismatches or to define the problems which must be solved if an organization is to get in tune with its environment. There is also the need to ensure that the solutions developed are imaginative and capable of ensuring a more healthy and profitable future for the company concerned. This is particularly true when the problem to be solved is the development of products or processes, or the penetration of markets which are entirely new to the company. Creative thinking and brainstorming techniques can be valuable in developing new ideas.

The task of coping with the changing business environment might, however, need a greater analytical and problem-solving capability than many firms possess. It is, therefore, worthwhile contemplating some of the ways in which a company's analytical and problem-solving capability might be extended.

The first option worth considering is the recruitment of additional staff of a high enough calibre to meet the company's needs. Ideally, these people should be experienced and should have demonstrated problem-solving and entrepreneurial capabilities of a high order. If such people can be found either externally, or perhaps internally (many organizations have capable people who are trapped in the system and have not been given the opportunity to exploit fully their talents), then this is the best solution. Unfortunately, as most companies are well aware, this is not always an easy option to take.

Another option is to employ external consultants. A number of management consulting firms maintain pools of highly talented problem solvers to find solutions to their clients' growth problems, which can include the design of new products on a sub-contract basis. This approach too can have a disadvantage: the people in a company who must implement any courses of action recommended by consultants are often loathe to commit themselves to the recommended solutions. All too often the consultants' report and recommendations become merely a document to be shelved rather than something to govern the company's future action.

A further option open to companies which is worthy of consideration is to draw on the talents available within the Higher Education system, for example in Business Schools, Regional Management Centres and Polytechnics. This is not to suggest that companies should call on academics to do the problem-solving. However, the combination of a group of managers who are keen to develop some part of their business and an academic who has had some practical business experience but who also has a wide knowledge of the various modern management techniques and approaches available and who understands the way in which learning can be encouraged can jointly provide a high powered diagnostic and problem-solving capability.

A group of managers from a nationalized group of companies assisted by staff of the Kingston Regional Management Centre carried out a detailed study of one of the transport companies in the group in order to recommend ways in which profitability could be improved. The combination of experienced managers and practically minded academics was able to produce recommendations for new strategies which, when implemented, had a significant effect on company profitability.

The organization structure

There is a strong connection between the organizational structure of a company and its ability to learn, to grow and to provide opportunities for the personal learning of the individuals making up the management team.

A bureaucratic type of organization structure in which jobs are carefully defined and relationships are prescribed provides little opportunity for innovation, creativity and personal development. In an organization of this kind, people's learning is focused generally on improving their professional excellence either in accountancy, production, marketing, or whatever particular function to which they belong. One problem with such an organization is that no one except the man at the top gives too much consideration to the business as a whole as distinct from its various components. Consequently, if the reasons why the business has succeeded in the past cease to exist because of the changing environment, then a company of this kind has great difficulty in learning what is needed to readjust its business or its activities to meet the current situation.

Another feature of such an organization is that people should obey rules and should 'know their place'. At certain stages in the development of a business this might be an important advantage. However, in coping with a changing environment this can be a distinct deterrent to taking the kind of risks and new initiatives which are important if a company is to establish a new direction for itself.

A bureaucratic organization can achieve impressive results when the tasks to be carried out are well known and the environment in which it is providing services is relatively stable. The penalty of such an organization structure is that it does not encourage the development of new ideas, new products or any kind of innovation that is likely to threaten the status quo. In fact, it is an organization structure which tends to focus both organizational and individual learning on prescribed and well explored topics. In the long run in a business environment which is changing rapidly an organization of the bureaucratic kind inevitably leads to low efficiency and can be in danger of becoming sufficiently out of touch with the needs of the real world as to threaten its survival.

A common form of organizational structure in industrial companies, particularly those which have developed from a successful single business idea, is that which divides a company into different functional departments. This structure, which can easily become bureaucratic, is illustrated in figure 4 below and is particularly common in companies in the UK.

Figure 4

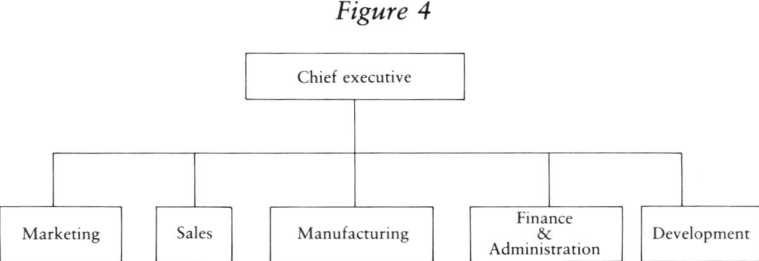

It is a structure which can be extremely successful where the business and the market it is serving are well known and relatively stable. The senior executive in a department is usually a specialist in the appropriate function. Other people in the department are strongly motivated towards increasing their competence in the specialism concerned since their promotion and other rewards will usually depend on it.

People in this type of organization become skilled at solving functional types of problems, eg production, marketing or finance problems. The centre of focus becomes the activities of their own department. Contacts with staff in other departments are limited and these people are often seen as competitors for resources or even as enemies who do not understand the difficulties and needs. Take, for example, the age old conflict between production and sales.

The barriers between departments can become extremely rigid and difficult to surmount. The sharing of experiences, knowledge and learning between departments can cease to exist. Consequently, although individual departments or sections might become more competent in coping with their problems, the organization as a whole does not increase its overall competence in dealing with the external world of business.

No one with the exception of the chief executive and possibly the corporate planner, if there is one, can see the business as a whole since it is only at their level that all the functions into which the business has been separated come together. Furthermore, it is often the case, particularly in larger companies, that the chief executive is too far removed from the 'action' to exercise other than a superficial influence on the way in which the business as a whole develops. The corporate planner often does not have sufficient influence in the organization to be a major factor in the situation.

In a firm manufacturing pneumatic and electronic control instruments, salesmen were frequently selling instruments to specifications which the production department had great difficulty in meeting and only then at considerable cost. This led to a continual conflict between the sales and manufacturing directors to the extent that they spoke to one another only when they had to. The managing director tried to resolve the conflict on the basis of personal relationships rather than on an objective assessment of the real problems involved. The accounting information provided by the finance director did not help to ascertain the true position.

Certain structures, distinct from the bureaucratic and functional structures described above, do encourage personal initiative and provide people with good opportunities for self actualization. Such structures have a more organic character, in other words, have less formalization. In organizations with such structures, the demands made on an individual are often more general and diffuse and reporting relationships are less specific and well defined than in the one-man-one-boss type of structure. Structures of this kind are more commonly found in some of the more recently established companies which have achieved success as a result of developing businesses based on advanced technology. Such companies more often than not will have a two or more dimensional matrix structure (*see* figure 5 on page 112) or perhaps some form of partial matrix.

Companies which are structured in this way will often be found to be suffering from a surfeit of innovative ideas and suggested changes rather than the reverse.

An interesting example of the use of the matrix structure comes from a major computer company. In the 20 odd years since it was founded the company has achieved an impressive growth record (turnover in 1979 was approaching three billion dollars), working with a multidimensional matrix structure for a number of years. One of the company's problems is not a lack of innovative ideas but rather the difficulty of selecting the most appropriate ones from the many being produced. This creativity and innovation is a prerequisite of success in the fast moving, high technology, computer based business areas in which the company is operating. It is an environment where the ability to identify new problems and to learn how to solve them is crucial to success.

It should not be thought that the choice of structure must lie between the extremes described. In fact, for many organizations an intermediate type of structure is appropriate. Others may require a collection of different structures which, in fact, might be essential for success in a complex and rapidly changing environment. Although innovation, creativity and learning about new things are essential in coping with a changing environment, there is also another important need. Once a promising business idea has been identified, there is then the need to ensure that it is properly developed to the stage where it has achieved sufficient penetration of the relevant market segments to generate cash which can be used in other parts of the business.

The way in which a company is structured can, therefore, have a profound effect on what a company is capable of learning and consequently on its capacity to cope with changing circumstances. The wrong kind of structure can prevent an organization from acquiring the new knowledge which might be essential for survival. This may mean that some way must be found to free people from the constraints imposed by their present positions in the organization.

A major Italian company manufacturing steel tubes was functionally organized with manufacturing units located in a number of different towns. Many key people, conditioned by the way the company had grown and was structured, saw the business as being that of manufacturing steel tubes for a variety of end uses. The company had been losing money for some time and management had attempted to cope with this problem without success by ringing the changes on more than one occasion between 'centralization' and 'de-centralization' of responsibility, and by numerous changes in manufacturing technology. It was only when a number of key executives were formed into teams to study what appeared to be appreciably different businesses in which the company was engaged (eg commercial tubes for domestic use, special high quality tubes for use in atomic power plants), that it was possible to establish the true, diverse nature of the company and to identify the real problems inhibiting the profitable development of the firm.

If the planning process is to be effective as the means for organizational learning, and hence for the kind of organizational change which leads to a real improvement in performance, it may be necessary to set up a planning activity which is outside the framework of the existing company structure. This activity could be considered an aspect of the 'transitional' management of the company, or that part of management which is concerned with assisting the company to change from one organizational arrangement to another. It is a form of management which is discussed more fully in chapter 9.

THE SYSTEM OF REWARDS AND PUNISHMENTS

An important aspect of any company is the system by which it rewards or punishes its personnel for success or failure in chosen paths. This system can have a profound effect on the direction in which learning takes place in an organization and on the extent to which individuals are prepared to get involved in learning.

As mentioned above, the bureaucratic structure in which the different activities concerned with a business are subdivided into many specialist functions often has the kind of reward system that encourages a person to climb the ladder within his or her own area of specialism. Although this can have its good side in that by the time a person, for example, becomes the head of production, he is well versed in all problems within the production field, it has an inherent disadvantage in that he may not on the other hand be fully aware of the part which production plays in the total business process.

Perhaps the most common example of how rewarding success in a limited direction can have an adverse effect on other desirable requirements is provided by many production incentive schemes. In a company manufacturing instruments for controlling temperature and pressure, the production operatives were paid for the number of instruments produced above a certain level. Here the focus was on numbers rather than quality; subsequent inspection found that many of the instruments produced had to be rejected for quality reasons. This, in turn, led to increased costs from either scrapping or reworking.

The reasons for which a company punishes its personnel also have an important influence on the company's learning. All too often a mistake leads to punishment rather than review in a more realistic light. In many organizations people are blamed for getting things wrong and this tends to discourage any attempts to be different or to break out in new directions. Although this might be desirable in some types of concern, in others where the problem is that of contending with the changing environment this brake on initiative taking can detract from the company's capability for coping.

The position of a government agency changed appreciably in relation to its clients once the colonies had achieved independence. This change of relationship meant that the company could no longer expect business to come in without effort; it had to go out and generate it, often in the face of intense competition. Many of the older people in the organization were reluctant to take the risk of trying to change things to cope with this new situation because of the past practice of blaming or punishing people for stepping outside established procedures.

An important feature of the system of incentives, rewards or punishments in a company, often overlooked, is that it strongly influences the company's system of values. The system indicates what should and what should not be done. A well designed system of incentives can, therefore, not only provide an important means of improving a company's level of performance, but can also be used to modify its value system.

However, where a company is operating in a changing business environment, what was good practice in one year may be inappropriate in the following year. Consequently it is all too common that a company's system of incentives is found to be geared to encouraging what was essential to success in the past but which is now no longer relevant. Clearly a consideration of the learning needs of a company cannot take place meaningfully unless some thought is also given to the system of rewards and punishments which the company is using either explicitly or implicitly.

> A Swedish firm manufacturing stainless steel slabs, plates and sheets had diversified its products to include a wide range of dimensions. A key operator in the manufacturing process was the man who handled the overhead crane at a critical intermediate storage point. He could select the next pieces of steel to be dispatched to later stages of processing. Unfortunately his incentive payments were based on the tonnage he transported which encouraged him to give priority to either the heavier pieces of steel or those which could easily be reached and moved. The lighter pieces of steel or those which had been covered by heavy plates and were difficult to reach tended to be left behind. The main effect of this practice was that priorities were assigned to meet the needs of the crane operator rather than the company's business and important orders were often delayed unnecessarily.

People needs versus company needs

One aspect of the growing maturity of a company is that more attention tends to be focused on shaping the organization to meet the needs, ambitions and demands of its key employees. This can be an important and desirable stage of development for a company, particularly as it is one way of gaining the commitment of employees to the objectives of the enterprise. It is dangerous, however, when this is done at the expense of those aspects of the problem-solving role of the organization which are concerned with helping the business to adapt to the changing needs of the environment. All too often there can be a reluctance to modify a company's business(es) to meet the changing needs of the market place in order to avoid interfering with the vested interests of the existing key people and skills. This situation is often likely to occur in the larger sized company where the adverse effects of this policy on company performance are more difficult to detect.

A senior member of the board of a major company in the chemical industry was seconded to a nationalized industry to carry out a major task of rationalization. The executive concerned initiated a reconsideration of the industry's activities which led to the closure of many loss making sections and a reallocation of available capital into activities which showed promise. The executive, who had hoped to rejoin his own company in the most senior position and to implement similar policies of reconstruction, found that the established power group were not prepared to allow him to return and carry them out.

Shortage of information

It is not uncommon for the initial fact finding studies to be inhibited by the absence of that information which is essential for a deep understanding of the company's real situation. There might be insufficient data about markets and market trends, and financial or cost information systems might not be sufficiently well developed to indicate how the company makes its money or loses it. An example is:

> In the case of the government agency mentioned on page 75, the development of plans to further its business getting

activity and to achieve commercial viability was inhibited by the lack of knowledge of the real needs of its potential clients and the activities that were profitable. In consequence, its early attempts to develop a viable corporate plan were of limited success until this information was obtained.

This lack of information, however, should not be allowed to delay the start of planning. Planning is a continuing cyclic process which initially may have to rely on good guesses where factual information is not available. The important requirement is that an effective planning process should be started. The initial fact finding and problem diagnostic stages in this process can then be used to identify further information needs and to assign priorities for its collection.

Continuing with the above example, a major part of the agency's earlier plans was to identify the kind of information that was necessary to help it understand its existing situation and then to prepare plans for collecting it.

Support from change agents

The need to think in analytical and evaluative terms about what is being done can be a painful experience for people accustomed to subduing their fears and doubts by engaging in action to the exclusion of reflection. They may need considerable support and encouragement if they are to do this in the early stages of getting involved in the planning. It is at this stage that the presence of an impartial 'change agent' can be particularly important.

The change agent might be a person within the company or alternatively an outsider who is helping the company to initiate and manage its change process. However, what is important is that he is recognized as someone who has the confidence of top management and who can both support and help to legitimate any attempt to go beyond existing boundaries. The boundaries in question can be either organizational ones or those concerned with the company's normal behaviour.

A number of successful projects have depended on the presence of both an internal and an external change agent who have developed a close working relationship with one another and also with a key member of the power group, preferably the recognized leader, in the organization concerned.

In the States of Jersey it was a group composed of the politician who was President of the two key committees responsible for strategic and organizational change, namely the Finance and Economics and the Establishment Committees; the Civil Servant responsible for Establishments, and one of the authors acting as an external consultant which played a significant part in the programme of change designed to create a Civil Service more in tune with the Island's future needs. This programme was implemented over a period of some seven years following an initial study which took about six months to complete.

The roles of the change agents will be described in greater detail in the next chapter. It is worth commenting here, however, that an important part of their roles should be to assist the planning groups to a clearer understanding of and to have a greater control over that part of the business environment which concerns them.

Importance of a 'whole business'

The importance of having study groups develop an understanding of a 'whole business' cannot be emphasized too much. Having people, preferably in multi-disciplinary teams, review a whole business in depth and develop plans for improving it gives them a perception of the totality of their business that is usually lacking at the outset. It helps them gain a better understanding of the contribution that they as individuals in their existing roles can make to the success of the business as a whole. This, in turn, often helps them to increase the effectiveness of their contribution.

Establishing the planning process

Once a planning process of the kind visualized has been initiated, it must be established as a continuing organizational process otherwise it can fade away. It is useful, therefore, to prepare a programme and timetable for setting up the planning process to which the people engaged in the project will attempt to work. This programme should set firm targets for completion of the various stages and should provide some incentive to participants to complete the stages on time. Although this approach relates here to the initial fact finding and planning stages when such a scheme is introduced, it applies equally to subsequent plans in later years. The review and planning process must become established as a continuing part of the company's procedures which should be conducted annually or perhaps at even shorter intervals.

If the planning process is to become an effective process for change then the programme should also:

(a) discuss the change process itself and its needs and requirements with the people who are involved in it
(b) communicate an understanding of what is happening to all people who need to know
(c) provide a means of managing the process.

It is here that the external and internal change agents can play a particularly useful role. They should be free to move about the organization at all levels of management and in all departments. They should use this freedom to inform people of the progress of the change process in other parts of the organization and to provide encouragement to those who either are having difficulty in appreciating the need for change or are uncertain about the usefulness of the contribution they, as individuals, can make to the change process.

The difficulty which is likely to be encountered as the planning process proceeds and becomes increasingly participative is that many of the managers taking part will have had little experience in analysing those parts of the company's situation outside their own departmental activities. In addition, many of them will be unfamiliar with the kind of analytical techniques which may be needed to investigate different aspects of the company's affairs. It may be important, therefore, to provide the fact finding and planning groups with some form of educational support.

It may be necessary to provide them with an understanding of fact finding techniques and how to analyse and interpret the data produced. This is a task which might be undertaken by the change agents or in some cases by the company's training department. It may, however, be necessary to import the required skills and experience either by drawing on the services of consultants or educational establishments of various kinds.

Some of the main contributions made by the staff of the Kingston Regional Management Centre to the study of a transport company, undertaken jointly with some of the company's own managers, were concerned initially with the provision of techniques for analysing the company's financial and product/market situation. Later, as the study progressed, they were able to help in defining the company's problems and suggesting methods for solving them.

Handling tensions

The process of adjusting and modifying the system of ideas and beliefs of a company can be influenced strongly by in-company tensions. These tensions, which can subject the system of ideas, etc to stresses of various kinds, can be generated by natural driving forces arising from mismatches between the company and its environment. On the other hand, they may result from the personal strategies chosen by key people in the company. These latter types of tension can play a significant part in building a company's capacity to grow and to renew itself providing the people generating the tensions are capable of surviving the personal stress which can be engendered.

Unless some form of tension is present it is unlikely that a change process of any kind will begin. Tension can play two parts in this connection. First it can create the necessary motivation for starting a change and secondly it can in many cases influence the direction in which the change takes place.

An important stage in the development of the Italian company manufacturing steel tubes mentioned earlier was the reorganization into a number of sub-businesses based on product groupings such as commercial tubes, special quality tubes, etc. Following a detailed appraisal of each of these sub-businesses management teams were appointed by the Director-General to develop them. The combination of the knowledge provided by the earlier fact finding exercise combined with the tension created by the demands of the Director-General for growth and profitability soon began to achieve positive results in accordance with the changed shape of the business.

Tension is also important in achieving growth or introducing innovation. At an early stage in the development of a growth process, effective planning should be based on the creation or exploitation of tension. (See R Normann). On the other hand, in the later stage of a growth process when an adequate share of the targetted market segments have been achieved, tensions or conflict of any kind are much less desirable.

In order to judge whether a tension or conflict is of value it is important to know its cause. A common type of conflict results when a company's organization structure is out of tune with its business ideas and thus fails to provide an appropriate support for an efficient exchange process. Conflicts of this type are rarely beneficial. On the other hand, conflicts which arise from tensions between diverging interpretations of the company's situation by key people in the power structure can be of potential benefit. This conflict at some stage must be resolved and doing so can result in the development of a more effective set of strategies.

THE KEY POWER GROUP

Some of the main barriers to learning and subsequent change will almost certainly exist in the key power group and the success of the process will depend on the extent to which these key figures can be influenced. This should be taken into account in organizing the fact finding activities. Periodic reviews with the main power group in which they can be helped to develop an up to date picture of the process as it progresses can help to influence the status quo forces which may exist. It can also provide the members of the power group concerned with a useful tool for influencing other interested parties in making further progress.

In a company providing various kinds of hygiene services it soon became apparent that one of the main bottlenecks to further progress and growth was the general manager and one of his senior colleagues. Periodic meetings were, therefore, arranged at which the study group concerned reviewed its findings with these executives. Comparing their findings with the established opinions and perceptions of the power group gradually helped the general manager to understand the way in which he was inhibiting the growth of the company, and helped him to develop a style of management which was more appropriate to achieving acceptable growth targets. It also helped him to develop a more realistic marketing policy in conjunction with his sales director based on a clearer understanding of the market which the company was attempting to exploit.

Gaining commitment to the process

The importance of gaining the commitment of senior executives to the continual process of fact finding, planning and change has already been stressed. It is important to ensure, however, that all groups which can affect the implementation of changes are in agreement about the present state of the organization, the problems which must be dealt with, the priorities which should be attached to these problems, and the policies and practices which will be adopted. This requires a continuing dialogue between the study and planning groups and these other groups. This is not only a process of helping the people in power to become concerned about the situation, but also of convincing them that an alternative plan of action to the present one will improve the situation for them and for others.

It is equally important to gain the commitment and involvement of the people actually forming the study/planning groups. The process should be organized so that personal growth and development becomes a real feature of the company's planning activities. This means that planning should proceed at a pace which allows sufficient time for the people involved to learn not only about the company's situation and deficiencies but also about their own development needs as individuals. The process should preferably be accompanied by a programme of learning geared to help the individuals to increase their competence in the work situation. This provides an incentive for the individuals concerned to become more deeply involved in the process. Allowance should also be made for the fact that many people will first need to discard their existing ideas and beliefs before they can assimilate more realistic and up to date ones.

Gaining commitment is often a case of providing people with an opportunity to 'do their own thing'. This can be particularly encouraging to people with entrepreneurial skills which they may not have had the opportunity to use in the past.

Considerable interest develops once participants in the working groups become aware that their work can lead to real changes in the organization which, in turn, helps to generate further momentum behind the process. It can create enthusiasm, release energy for problem solving and can help to increase involvement and flexibility. However, it should also be appreciated that enthusiasm can be overdone and it may be necessary from time to time to review the situation by monitoring the analyses to ensure that the problems have been defined correctly.

Many of the ideas for change that will come out of the planning groups may not be new. Someone in the organization will have thought of them already, but may never have been able to get these ideas through to, or accepted by, someone who has the power to initiate action.

In a quasi-government organization the planning groups

were particularly encouraged in their fact finding and later planning stages because the chief executive reviewed their findings, their conclusions and their recommendations for change with them. These reviews represented a major change in management style within the organization. They provided many members of the planning groups with their first opportunity of bringing their problems to the attention of someone in the organization who had sufficient power to take corrective action.

The development of teams

An important feature of the process desribed above is the formation of teams of people charged with responsibility for examining various aspects of the business. But what is a 'team' and how should the members be chosen and developed?

A team is much more than a collection of individuals who are jointly charged with a series of tasks. It is a careful mixture of skills and personalities which, combined, will achieve far more than they would individually. A great deal has been written about team development and it is no part of the purpose of this book to repeat all the detail of successful team development. The bibliography sets out further reading for those who are interested. The following paragraphs highlight a number of points and show how they can be translated into successful practice through the exercise of basic management skill.

First there are four major potential problems which need to be resolved before a small group of people can perform as an effective team:

1 The team acts not as a team, but as a series of individuals each concerned with his/her own personal career and interests.
2 The team is compartmentalized. The individuals see themselves as representing their basic function and furthering its well-being rather than that of the team as a whole.

3 The team has objectives which are unclear or not accepted by the team members.
4 The team attempts to cope with the wrong problem. For example, it may be considering how to expand sales of existing products when the need is to develop a new product.

There are also three prime needs of successful team working:

1 The team must consist of capabilities appropriate to the problems to be solved.
2 The team may require to be changed or modified as its work progresses. As new ideas develop some members may need to be replaced by others who will have the responsibility for implementation at a later date. This will ensure that when the time comes they will 'own' the new ideas and have a vested interest in their success. Too often good ideas fail because of the 'not invented here' syndrome.
3 The team leader's role is crucial. He needs to be someone who has the personal capability of managing the various steps needed to solve the problem even though at an early stage he may not have the direct power to do so.

The team leader needs other personal skills. Of the many discussed in the literature perhaps three are crucial:

1 the ability to draw ideas out from people
2 the ability to listen to what they have to say
3 the ability to summarize contributions so that the whole team can move forward together.

Choosing an appropriate team requires thought. The Industrial Training Research Unit at Cambridge has carried out some interesting work on how to choose teams so that there is a blend of skill and personality which will optimize performance. The following checklist of questions offers some guide:

(a) Have I selected a team leader who has the necessary skills and personality and who will command respect?
(b) Have I included people who *together* have all the necessary technical knowledge, or who recognize the need to supplement their knowledge as necessary?

(c) Are there people on the team who between them will:
  i be able to identify and resolve problems
  ii formulate new, often radical, approaches
  iii lend stability by questioning way-out ideas
  iv be able to formulate action plans
  v ensure that the team keeps to a time-table and achieves its aims
  vi question whether the team has sufficient facts
  vii have enough experience of business and the industry to prevent the team ending up in 'cloud cuckoo land'?

The team will learn how to work together by working on problems. Part of the team leader's job is to build on and to use the skills he has available in the team. His guiding principle should be that the team has been formed not just to examine problems, but provide information and to make recommendations. Essentially its role is to make decisions and to take responsibility for action.

It is because the team has to achieve business results that its focus must be on action. There can be no place for minority reports. Every member must in the end come to terms with the fact that action has to be taken and that he has a personal contribution to make to the success of that action.

Tasks should be allocated to each member and should be carried out between meetings. The tasks vary between ascertaining facts and writing papers proposing courses of action or developing concepts. A team's success relies primarily on a commitment to hard work by each individual.

When setting up the fact finding and planning groups it should be appreciated that a major objective is to educate a large part of the organization in the company's situation and problems. It is essential to encourage the development of an open-minded view of the situation which is free from preconceived ideas. It is also useful to link the study groups with a senior member of management as this can be a way of ensuring that the findings of the groups are communicated to the company's board at an early stage. This can help to give the board advance warning of changes in strategy and policies which the groups may subsequently recommend.

The planning groups should be helped to understand the problem of resistance to change so that their plans can reflect consideration of the need to overcome it. Consequently, once the groups have decided on the kind of plans which must be implemented to achieve agreed goals, consideration should be given to the change process whereby these plans will be introduced.

Often the help a group needs is in removing obstacles which are preventing it from moving forward to a position of greater confidence.

A study group which was investigating the affairs of a company engaged in transporting containers between Scotland and Northern Ireland became frustrated and discouraged and was unable to understand how the company was making or losing its money. The change agent working with this group introduced it to a variation on the standard approach to break-even analysis which, when applied to the company's affairs, showed that once a certain level of traffic had been passed, the company began to lose money rather than to increase its profits by subsequent increases in the volume of business. This arose because of the imbalance in the volume of goods being transported between Scotland and Ireland resulting in the need to return empty containers to Scotland which caused operating costs to increase. This finding helped the group to bring its study to a successful conclusion.

It should be appreciated that it is the study group itself and the individuals in it which are the more important and not the particular problems with which they are dealing. The aim should not be merely to solve a problem but to help the group to develop its problem-solving confidence and capability so that it can cope with problems in a more integrated fashion. This aspect of group development is something to which the change agents should pay particular attention.

7
The change agents

It is clear that promoting change in an organization is not a straightforward or easy process. The barriers to change are too in-built for that to be the case. However, experience shows that the combination of an executive who wields real power, an internal change agent who is respected, and an external catalyst who understands his role, is a combination which is almost irresistible in creating the environment in which effective change can take place. This chapter examines the role of these three figures in promoting change, and discusses some of the personal skills which adroit change agents deploy.

These three key figures, working together, are capable of promoting organizational change. Their roles are complementary. Each one has a unique contribution:

(a) the key executive to stimulate action and to invest that action with credibility
(b) the internal change agent to provide the drive and organizational flair which translate the key executive's stimulus into effective operation
(c) the external change agent to bring a wide view to the process, capable of raising sensitive issues, but aware that only the organization's executives are capable of supplying the answers.

Role of the Change Agents

Overall, the major role of a change agent is to stimulate learning within the organization so that it is capable of adapting on a continuing basis to the environment in which it operates. The momentum for any worthwhile activity is generated by senior people who are known to be committed to that activity. Normally the chief executive is the individual who stimulates thought and action. There are, however, organizations where another senior manager may have greater real power. The reasons why this can happen have no relevance to this book; it is sufficient to recognize the reality that in any organization there is an instinctive awareness of who wields real power and influence. It is that person whose support is critical to the success of any effective change process.

The reason for this is obvious. For the ideas in this book to succeed many people are required to invest time. 'We think it is a good idea but we haven't the time' is a common plea. The statement would be more honest if it were rephrased: 'we think it is a good idea in theory, but not sufficiently high on our list of priorities to devote time to it'.

Time is a function of priorities – not of hours and minutes available. There is never sufficient time to do all the things that could be done. In reality we do things we deem to be important. High on the list of such items are those which we think the boss will commend. This is why the active support of the key executive is so important. If people believe that he is behind the activity which comprises organizational learning then people will devote time and effort to discovering ways of making new ideas work. If they do not believe that there is any high level commitment, phrases such as: 'we've thought of all this before, but nothing ever changes round here' will be common currency.

The *key executive* provides the stimulus. He may also authorize the use of resources and take an active part in discussions. These latter aspects are less critical to success than the widespread recognition that he approves of the fundamental thinking which will result in the organization maintaining its congruence with its environment.

The role of the *internal change agent* is different. His contribution is to stimulate learning by his fellow executives and often to act as a scribe or recorder of their deliberations. He may assemble factual information and draft reports on their activities. In some areas he will have a contribution of his own to make, though his primary responsibility is to promote thought by his peers. There is no stereotype of an ideal internal change agent. The essential skills are similar but backgrounds can be many and varied. An agent may be old or young, of long service or relative newness, and may come from anywhere in the organization: finance, production, marketing or sales, personnel or training and so on. What is essential is that he should have the respect of his colleagues.

For a change agent respect is earned because he has the reputation of helping his colleagues; being more interested in their problems than in bemoaning his own difficulties; being a calming influence, lacking impetuosity, in short, being the sort of person who gets things done without making a big fuss about it or puffing up his own achievements. These are crucial qualities but they are not uncommon. Most organizations have someone like that for, although sometimes their abilities are overlooked, they make an essential contribution. Unfortunately the qualities of some change agents are recognized only after they have moved on and their presence is missed.

The person selected is likely to be a natural 'teacher', more concerned with formulating and suggesting the correct questions than with stressing his own answers or point of view. He must be trusted not to disseminate widely any indiscretions or confidential remarks uttered by the team with which he is working. Real progress is made by people revealing their true thoughts and feelings and they will be wary of doing this if they suspect that what they say in haste will be reported at leisure to more senior executives. Thus, people holding positions of 'assistant' may be unsuitable in certain organizations, more because of their position than because they lack the essential qualities referred to previously.

In summary, the ideal internal change agent is the sort of person who is always welcome when he drops into your office, or whom you naturally turn to when you want to talk over a problem.

External change agents are essentially catalysts. Some external advisors mistake this role. Primarily they should be concerned with the *process* of change. Any contribution they make to the *content* of discussions is a bonus, albeit sometimes an important one. Because external change agents have a wide experience of many organizations and situations, they should be capable of drawing on this experience to assist people to raise the quality of their thought about the issues of concern to the company. A guiding principle for all external change agents should be:

> Remember the problems you are dealing with are the organization's problems not your own. Therefore, your role is to help people in the organization to solve their own problems, not to solve them for them.

This demands great self-restraint. Too often the outsider is regarded as 'an expert' who has all the answers. People tend to do what he suggests. After all, if it does not work it is easy to blame him. There are many instances of outsiders who peddle panaceas or packages which have worked in one situation, but do not work in many others. An organization will develop only if it thinks through its problems and solutions for itself. The external change agent can assist but he is certainly no universal 'expert'.

Therefore, the twin roles of an external change agent are to facilitate the process of change through provoking thought on fundamental, and often sensitive issues, and by offering his own knowledge for consideration by the organization for which he is working. But only the organization can determine if that knowledge is relevant to their needs; only the executives in a company can initiate action.

There are many external change agents to choose from. They may be consultants in further education, from business schools, from industrial training boards from professional counselling companies and so on. Often they will wish to work on a part-time basis over a substantial calendar period. In this way their catalytic effect can be sustained without danger of their becoming so imbedded in the organization that they take on the role of an extra, but expensive, executive.

It is essential to think through the role of the external change agent before he is engaged. This should be made explicit both to him and to the organization. He must have access to all relevant information. He needs this if he is to obtain a true picture of the present situation so that he can formulate the correct questions. If you feel that you cannot trust your potential external change agent with confidential information then he is not the right man, whatever his other qualities.

These qualities are similar to those discussed in relation to internal change agents. Essentially he must be capable of earning respect rapidly and be a natural 'teacher'. A good external change agent is one who is capable of helping an organization to create situations from which it can learn.

THE SKILLS OF INTERNAL CHANGE AGENTS

Whatever their background, change agents need to possess a number of key skills. The list below, which is drawn up mainly for the benefit of internal change agents, is not intended to be exhaustive but deals only with those skills which have been found to be essential. They include the ability to:

(a) identify and to isolate problems
(b) discriminate between fact and fiction
(c) systematize data
(d) listen – as opposed to hearing only
(e) ask the right question at the right time
(f) summarize a discussion
(g) remain silent
(h) make verbal presentations
(i) write persuasively
(j) help individuals and groups to acquire confidence.

Since many of these skills are dealt with in detail in other publications they are discussed only briefly here.

The ability to identify and to isolate problems

A great deal has been written about problem solving. At one extreme there is the thesis that a problem is a deviation from a normal or expected situation. On the other hand de Bono suggests that the 'no problem' situation may often be a problem because one ought to be searching for a better way. This is the antithesis of 'letting well alone'. In the middle there is the vast area of difficulty in distinguishing between a real problem, about which one ought to be doing something, and irritants, about which one can do little or nothing.

In one important sense problem identification is the ability to recognize that whatever the outside constraints there are still opportunties for improvement, for doing things differently. The ability of an organization to adapt, and therefore, to survive, depends on a recognition that despite the well understood constraints there remain practical possibilities for doing things differently.

A change agent possesses the skill to help his colleagues to find a way to understand the real nature of the problems they encounter. To do this he needs to be able to:

(a) stress that problems often arise because objectives, or what people are trying to achieve, are unclear. Clarify the objective and then the real problem often isolates itself
(b) understand that problem identification may be a matter of reordering existing information, that is, laying more stress on certain known factors than on the ones traditionally thought to be important
(c) identify when new information is required and, equally, when sufficient is already available. This is an important skill because the search for new information is often used as an excuse for not being able to think rationally about the facts already prossessed
(d) see behind an apparent problem to its root causes. The so-called problem may be only a manifestation of a deeper underlying situation.

A successful internal change agent uses these insights to assist his colleagues to develop their own thinking. To do this he uses the skills of questioning and summarizing which are discussed in more detail later. At this stage all that need be said is that:

(a) clear thinking about what one is trying to achieve
(b) the isolation of real, as opposed to apparent, problems
(c) a determination not to discuss solutions before clarifying what is to be resolved

all represent the hallmarks of successful problem solving.

The ability to discriminate between fact and fiction

The tendency to over-simplify, or to generalize in the field of problem identification, has already been described. Myths are important and necessary ingredients in organizational thinking because they may supply the drive to achieve success. 'We are the best' at something may not be accurate, but it should provide a spur to improvement.

On the other hand 'we are the best' may lull an organization into a false sense of complacency. Ask yourself these questions about your company:

(a) why do we think our customers buy from us rather than from another supplier?
(b) if we are honest do we really live up to the image we think our customers have of us?
(c) what are the changes we should consider if we are to safeguard in the future our customers' image of us?

If you find that you are able to answer these questions coolly and dispassionately then you are likely to be capable of discriminating between fact and fiction.

A successful change agent is well aware that his organization has its own myths. He must be capable of exposing them when they interfere with the process of keeping the organization's policies and systems compatible with the real world. This does not mean that he must expose all the organization's myths because some are of value in fostering a sense of well-being and security. He also needs the skill and the tenacity to understand that even an exposed myth will not bring a general acceptance of a need for change. 'Don't confuse me with facts – I've made my mind up' is not just a cliché, it represents a deeply rooted prejudice held by someone about something in every organization.

A change agent needs the skill, experience and understanding to know how to deal with this all too common situation. He should also realize that when people discover things for themselves they are more likely to believe them than when they are 'told' that myths are really myths. So, even when he suspects that fiction is not being separated from fact he will be wiser to ask questions which will lead those responsible to a greater understanding of reality, than to uncover the facts himself and gleefully present them to a sceptical or hostile manager.

The ability to systematize data

Reordering existing information is an essential ingredient for determining the optimum changes in policy or practice which may be required. First however, there is a need to collect facts, and when these have been assembled, to order or present them in a way which will most readily enable people to draw inferences from them.

It has been suggested earlier that data collection is often, though not invariably, best organized by managers themselves because discovering for oneself is a major way of learning to come to terms with reality. Where data is collected by a number of managers it needs to be collated and presented in a form which aids interpretation.

The internal change agent often has a major role to play in this process. Much time can be wasted at meetings by the participants attempting to draw inferences from incompatible basic information. A little prior thought can avoid much fruitless discussion. The change agent should be capable of anticipating this type of situation and suggesting means of overcoming it.

A typical sequence is for a group to determine what information it will require for its next meeting. The change agent needs to ask:

(a) Will we be comparing like with like?
(b) If what we are comparing is not identical, will the

differences invalidate the conclusions we may wish to draw?
(c) If different measuring rules are in use, which one should we use as a basis and how can we most readily convert other scale measurements to the one we have chosen?

These, and similar questions, should be posed to the group before they go away and assemble data. Indeed, the change agent can often perform a useful service by preparing proformae for members of the group to fill in. Form design is a subject outside the scope of this book but references can be found in the bibliography.

A final warning. When the data is presented for interpretation the change agent would be wise to ask:

What does this mean?

rather than offering his own conclusions. By this means he will be helping people to come to terms with reality by ensuring that they draw the (often) unpalatable conclusions for themselves.

The ability to listen

The ability to listen well is perhaps the most demanding skill for the change agent to develop. Listening is by no means the same thing as hearing and then commenting on what one has heard. Listening is the ability to:

(a) absorb the ideas which are being expressed
(b) assess their significance
(c) be aware of any 'hidden agendas' which are implied but not being overtly declared
(d) relate what is being said to ideas which either the speaker or someone else has developed previously
(e) latch on to any key phrases or ideas, and retain them for future use if desirable.

This is a great deal to do at once. Fortunately, it is not an impossible task, although it does demand much concentration and is, therefore, tiring, particularly when one is learning to listen attentively.

Because our brains are capable of processing the obvious

meaning of words much faster than the speaker delivers them we have 'spare time' while listening in the everyday sense of that word. Learning to listen well is concerned primarily with learning how to use this 'spare time' most effectively. Consider some of the things we do in normal life when listening:

(a) our attention wanders because we have heard it all before
(b) we assess whether we agree or disagree with what the speaker is saying
(c) we develop our own response to be used as soon as the speaker stops talking. If he goes on too long we may even interrupt
(d) we hear only superficially and continue to develop our own thinking, possibly even considering what a previous speaker has said.

If you don't believe this just consider the points next time you have a conversation with someone.

Taking notes is the simplest method of learning to listen. The act of writing forces the listener to assess the meaning behind the words spoken. It concentrates the listener's mind on what is essential and focuses his attention on what may have been missed or deliberately left unsaid. Like any other skill, learning to listen demands concentration and practice. Once acquired, it will increase markedly the capacity to derive meaning and purpose from discussions.

Without this skill change agents find that they miss or overlook many chances to act as a true catalyst. As with so much else, timing is all important in promoting change in people's attitudes. The right question at the auspicious moment; the reference to something which has gone before; the summary which encapsulates an idea or clarifies an argument, are all dependent on the ability to listen well.

The ability to ask the right questions

Asking the correct question at the moment when it is likely to have the greatest impact is the next important skill. Everyone can ask questions, but few ask them after a process of thought which formulates exactly the type of question which is likely to develop the discussion in a constructive direction.

When we ask a question we set the thought pattern of our listeners in a certain direction. The indiscriminate asking of questions can retard the useful progress of a conversation because it may cut across the development of a line of thought in the listeners' minds which would have led in a useful direction. Yet how often do we hear people in ordinary conversation ask questions which can have no other purpose than indiscriminate curiosity on the part of the questioner?

Most people ask questions to satisfy their own thought needs. If they discover the answer then their own process of thought moves forward. This should not be the primary purpose of asking a question on the part of a change agent. His skill lies in asking questions which will lead his hearers to develop their thought patterns. Next time you take part in a meeting spend a little time listening to the questions asked by other people and ask yourself whether they help the meeting forward, or are asked only to satisfy the needs of the questioner.

The three major types of question are:

1 closed
2 open
3 leading

The closed question places reasonably tight constraints on the response, eg 'did you make a profit last year?' The open question allows the responder greater freedom in how he answers, eg 'tell me about your profit position last year?'. The leading question suggests a line of response which may not have occurred to the responder, eg 'what were the major factors contributing to your profitability last year?'.

Each type of question can be useful. No one type is to be preferred in general to any other. What is important is to be capable of formulating and asking the right type of question at the moment when it will be most helpful in moving a discussion forward. There can be no rules about this because all discussions are different and so are all the people taking part in them. Here, however, are a few examples:

(a) closed questions can be used to elicit facts, eg how many? what type? where?

(b) open questions allow the participants to explore new areas and to expand their thought patterns, eg what would happen if . . .? (used to stimulate lateral thinking); why?

(c) leading questions push the discussion in a specific direction, eg what are the benefits we get from . . .? what are the reasons for . . .?

Clearly, there is a degree of overlap between the different types of question. This is of no consequence because we are not in the business of categorizing questions. We *are* in the business of thinking through, before we ask a question, the likely effect of this question on the thought patterns of our listeners.

The ability to summarize

Summarizing is perhaps one of the great under used skills. All good chairmen summarize discussions at regular intervals because they know that this is the way to keep discussions wandering from the point at issue. Most general conversations tend to wander in an uncontrolled manner because the participants follow each other's thought patterns without bothering to relate what is being said to the original aspect of the subject under discussion. Summarizing is the province of a good chairman and also of a good change agent. His job is to help a group of people to develop their thinking. He can aid them by summarizing their conversation regularly so that each person can relate his own thinking to the progress being made by the group.

The taking of notes is an important aid in being able to summarize. Some people advocate summarizing on a flip chart and this is often helpful. The act of summarizing often illuminates aspects which have been missed or which require more development. For the change agent the discipline involved in preparing to summarize regularly is helpful in that he is forced to understand where the group's thinking has arrived. This will make it more difficult for him to impose his own thinking on the group except when they have lost impetus and direction.

The ability to remain silent

For the change agent silence has a special significance. He may remain silent because he is so busy listening and taking notes that he has no time, or will, to intervene verbally. This kind of silence is readily understood and requires no further elaboration.

However, there is a type of silence which is difficult to cope with and demands skill and patience on the part of the change agent. This is the type of silence that occurs when a person, or people, are thinking about what has just been verbalized. People find such silences embarrassing and normally rush into say something just to maintain the flow of words.

A change agent needs to recognize that if he terminates a silence when other people are thinking he destroys at a stroke their pattern of thought because they will turn their attention to what he has just said. In practice this wastes time. Records of conversation show clearly that when interruptions of this kind take place it may be as much as 20 minutes before the original point, which was in the thinker's mind, is enunciated.

We need to guard against such phrases as 'What I mean is . . .' or similar silence destroyers if we are to encourage real thought. The careful observation of a thinker's facial expression, and the slowing down of his rate of speech may be important indicators that he is 'thinking'. Next time you are in a meeting note down the number of occasions on which someone destroys a silence, when allowing it to continue might have served a more useful purpose. The ability to remain silent demands great self discipline and it is an invaluable asset.

The ability to make verbal presentations

Any study group is likely to have to make a verbal presentation, possibly to the company's board or chief executive, on the results of its deliberations. Although the change agent working with the group may not make the presentation himself he should be capable of ensuring that it is of a high professional standard. This implies that he, himself, possesses the competence to make such a presentation.

The basis of a sound verbal presentation is adequate preparation. In order to prepare sufficiently it is necessary to have a clear understanding of what message one is trying to implant in the receiver's mind. This means starting to prepare from the hearer's viewpoint and not the speaker's.

So the first question to determine is what does the listener expect to hear? The answer to this question may bear little resemblance to that which the speaker wishes him to understand. No matter, it is still the starting point for the presentation because a verbal presentation is in effect a learning experience. To learn one has to start with what one knows, or thinks one knows, and build up an argument from there. It is no use starting somewhere else even if it would be better, or more realistic, to start from there. This is because we live in a real world of a mixture of facts, myths and prejudices, and the presenter has to take account of all three.

The speed with which an argument can be developed varies. It is boring to have to listen to what one knows, or thinks one knows; it is confusing to be expected to make leaps which omit important stages in the development of an idea. There is no rule of thumb method for determining how fast one should go, other than to be aware of the difficulty and to keep thinking about the problem from the listener's viewpoint. Facial or other body indicators will give clues during the presentation and these will suggest modifications to the prepared script which take account of the audience's learning needs.

The ability to summarize stages of the argument, to modulate one's voice, to use visual aids and so on are all aspects of sound verbal presentation. The reader will find references which explore these matters in detail in the bibliography.

The key, however, is to think about one's presentation from the audience's point of view and not one's own. What do they expect to hear? What do I want them to learn? How can we fill that gap? These are the three essential questions which form the basis of sound preparation.

The ability to write persuasively

Verbal messages, however competently delivered, are by their very nature ephemeral. They require to be complemented by the written word and this is likely to take the form of a report on the study group's work which is intended to persuade the reader to take, or to authorize, some specific action.

Such reports are not easy to write. The strength of the message has to convince the reader of the correctness of the advice and of its superiority over any other course of action. It has also to stimulate the action once the need for it has been accepted.

Any piece of writing fulfils its purpose when the reader has interpreted it and acted upon it precisely as the writer intended. The responsibility for achieving this result is entirely the writer's. He has only the written word as a tool and he must use it in a way that ensures the clarity, impact and continuity of his message. Again the bibliography indicates references for the reader to develop the skills of written communication.

The ability to write well demands practice and criticism, especially self-criticism. Those who are good writers, and will take the trouble, find that they are able to wield an influence which is an essential hallmark of an effective change agent.

The ability to help others to acquire confidence

All managers have constructive views on ways in which improvements could be made in their jobs. Many of these they are able to put into effect themselves, but for some important areas they recognize that they require resources which it is not within their power to provide. In these cases they make proposals to their superiors which are often turned down. The reasons given for rejection may be sketchy or detailed, but the manager is often left with the impression that, somehow, he has failed because his superiors do not recognize the overwhelming merit of his ideas and, therefore, of himself.

In some companies the situation is made worse when outside consultants are engaged. Every manager knows of cases where apparently the consultants have listened to ideas and remodelled them in a report, which has then been accepted and implemented by senior management. The cry goes up, 'why did they not take my advice in the first place and save money on those expensive outsiders?'. It is useless to talk of the prophets not being listened to in their own country; the managers feel that their own worth has been devalued by their superiors.

These comments are prompted by the experience of many consultants working with groups of managers and with individual managers over the years. Too often for comfort, employees say that there is no point in their recommending a first class idea because their own superiors will take no notice. The consultants, as the outside prophets, should take the matter up for them, they say. This attitude may be realistic, but it is certainly dangerous and does the company no good because the strength of a company depends on its own managers, not on the abilities of outsiders.

Outside change agents as well as internal ones have an important role to play as indicated in the last chapter. This role certainly does not include doing anything which devalues the standing of existing managers. Indeed, one of the major abilities of a change agent should be his capacity to help those with him to develop their confidence. By achieving this he will gain the satisfaction of knowing that his intervention may have some lasting effect for good.

This ability to help others to develop is difficult to define because it does not spring from a series of mechanistic actions. It is based, rather, on a number of attitudes, chief of which is the satisfaction derived from seeing someone else doing well. Indeed, a change agent's major sense of achievement should come when the people he is helping wonder what use he was because the managers themselves seem to have done it all.

8
How one company learned to cope

This chapter describes how one company managed its learning by making use of a strategic planning process to cope with some of the adverse consequences of major changes in its business environment. It also illustrates many of the issues raised in the foregoing chapters and describes the practical steps taken by the company in dealing with them. The company's success lay in the fact that it had the will to re-think its approach to business and took the action necessary to come to terms with what was in effect a new and different environment. This required an understanding of its position and a response to the opportunities and threats presented by its changed environment. In the process, it recognized that it had become a different kind of business and had the courage to make major revisions to its structure and to adopt more participative working methods to cope with the new situation. It also rid itself of the belief that its business success was tied to a particular trade.

BACKGROUND

The company was a medium size firm manufacturing and marketing textile fabrics. It was, and still is, a wholly owned subsidiary of a major textile group. Before the project described began it was losing money. The company was, and had been, keen on growth; over the past few years manufacturing capacity and turnover had more than doubled. The increase in capacity was a response to success in the field of apparel fabrics.

Manufacturing resources were located on two sites. On one site manufacturing shared the same building as the Head Office which contained the sales, product development, administrative and financial control functions. The firm's growth in manufacturing capacity had taken place on a second site in a development area. This expansion had taken place in two stages, the second of which had just been completed at the start of the project.

The chief executive was a keen innovator and had strong leanings towards a participative system of management. The management team was composed of young and enthusiastic executives who were committed to making a success of the business. The company had a functional organization structure with sales, production, product development and finance as the main functions.

The company saw its business as manufacturing, dyeing, finishing and marketing fabrics mainly for use in fashion orientated industries. The end uses of the fabrics were primarily in men's, women's and children's apparel. However, it had become increasingly evident that there were other markets available for its fabrics in which the aesthetic limitations on its products imposed by the technology of production were less of a constraint. As a result, the company was beginning to produce more and more fabrics for industrial uses of various kinds, although these were seen as ancillary to their use in various types of garment. One particular development of interest was the use of fabrics for car seat upholstery. This development had been pushed by the development director initially, against resistance from other senior people in the company. Although the importance of this market was now recognized, there was still resistance to its acceptance frm those whose 'main' experience had been with more traditional fabric end uses.

The problems of the company

The increase in manufacturing capacity coincided with a major downturn in demand from the company's traditional markets. Consequently, the company increased sales volume but at the expense of profit margins which were also eroded by inflation. Given the state of the market the company was unable to recover its increased costs.

In an attempt to improve the profit position the company became involved in an increasing number of new products and markets, such as fabrics for industrial and household uses, eg curtains. Business with the automobile industry also continued to expand and make a profit. However, the accounting system was not structured to inform the company of the relative profitability of its various products. Faced with a shortfall in working capital and considerable growth in the volume of business it was unable to identify which sectors of the business were making money or which were using the most capital.

A particularly serious problem was that its learning was insufficiently focused. Its marketing people were learning a small amount about many different market segments and not enough about any of them to exploit them properly. There was a lack of knowledge and understanding of many of the markets being served which meant that a number of areas with considerable potential were being neglected.

The top management team recognized that the business environment in which they were operating was changing rapidly. They appreciated that the company had to concentrate its efforts into fewer, carefully chosen market segments but appreciated that its knowledge of the environment was insufficient to allow this to be done effectively. Management was uncertain about which problems needed to be solved first in order to achieve an adequate level of profits. However, they were prepared to explore all possible options. In consequence, all the senior executives had become highly action orientated: 'having lost sight of their objectives, they redoubled their efforts'. Many of them worked long hours of overtime and were prepared to devote an exceptional amount of their personal talents to attempting to solve the company's problems.

PRELIMINARY SOUNDINGS

The chief executive decided to appoint an external adviser to help the senior executives both to see their problems in a different light and also to develop an integrated plan of improvement which would make the company viable. The chief executive, the external advisor and the director with responsibility for corporate planning then developed proposals for undertaking a programme of joint problem solving and learning for agreement by the executive board. They proposed that three groups of managers should be chosen to investigate the following areas of the company's business:

(a) fabrics for men's, women's and children's wear
(b) automotive and industrial fabrics
(c) household fabrics.

The groups consisted of four people from different disciplines in the company and each one was headed by a member of the board.

The study groups were chosen by the board taking care that all senior members of management with a significant role in the company were included. Each group was asked to study the allotted business area with the objectives of:

(a) developing an understanding of the nature of the business or businesses in the chosen area
(b) identifying the marketing, manufacturing and financial aspects of these businesses, also their profitability and usage of working capital
(c) determining the problems and barriers to further profitable growth.

A timetable was set for the investigations and it was agreed that the external advisor would meet each study group at about fortnightly intervals. It was further decided that the groups would be allowed four months to carry out their studies after which they would be expected to present their findings to the other senior members of management.

Each group was staffed with representatives from the main functions of marketing, production, product development and accounting. The executive directors selected to head the groups were chosen because they were responsible for the three main functions which would be affected by changes; namely, marketing, production and product development.

Fact finding and diagnosis

Each group was set the task of finding answers to the questions listed in the appendix on page 135 related to the business areas they were asked to study.

The time originally allowed for this study had to be extended, as it was soon realized that the company's understanding of its various markets was extremely limited. This particularly applied to the apparel fabrics which generated most of the company's income.

The major conclusions reached were:

(a) that the company was engaged in what could be regarded as five different businesses (ie five different business ideas were identified)
(b) that if the company was to fulfil its obligations to its major customer for automotive fabrics, then the volume produced would need to double at least in the following year
(c) that this particular business was capital intensive and that the company would run short of working capital unless more funds were made available.

During the fact finding stage members of the study groups began to develop an understanding of the business issues of the company as distinct from their own departmental affairs. This created an enthusiasm for continuing the project and for solving the problems which had been identified.

Planning and problem solving

Next it was decided that planning groups would be set up to prepare plans for developing four of the different businesses identified in the earlier stage. A member of the executive board was allocated to work with each group and give them such help as was needed. However, they were not expected to fulfil a leadership role. Each group was allocated two permanent members, a group leader who would be responsible subsequently for developing the business and a representative from the product development function. Each group was asked to prepare a planning report covering the following issues:

(a) a restatement of the business idea
(b) the criteria for achieving success and how this should be met
(c) external and internal environmental factors affecting the business
(d) a definition of the problems and barriers inhibiting profitable growth
(e) agreed objectives for the business over the next three years
(f) opportunities available to the business and environmental threats
(g) recommended strategies
(h) plans for solving the problems and achieving the agreed objectives
(i) additional resources required
(j) likely results of the plans.

Important features of this stage of the study were that:

(a) growth and profit objectives were agreed between the chief executive and the groups
(b) constraints on implementation likely to be presented by the existing organizational structure were identified and corrections suggested.

Approximately four months were allowed for preparing these plans. This stage of the project ended with the group leaders making presentations to the chief executive and other executive directors.

Implementing the plans

When completed the plans were agreed with the chief executive, following which the leader of each group was appointed as manager and given responsibility for implementing them. A central group was set up, headed by the chief executive, to facilitate implementation of the plans and to overcome obstacles outside the control of the business managers. This group paid particular attention to accelerating the product development programme as this had been identified as one of the main company bottlenecks.

A review was made two months after implementation began in order to assess progress and to identify any constraints that were being imposed by the organization structure. The review was carried out with each business area manager by a planning committee consisting of the managing director, the marketing director, the financial controller and the director responsible for product development. One of the main tasks of this committee was to allocate priorities in relation to the product development programme. It was also responsible for resolving conflicts between the business groups for other scarce resources so that the allocations fulfilled company, rather than narrow sectional, requirements. This activity resulted in the development of a matrix structure for the company which is illustrated in figure 5 below.

The workings of this revised organization were facilitated by the work done during the initial fact finding stage of the project. At that time the need to work in multi-functional groups had led to informal relationships between people from different functions which had helped them to appreciate better their own and others' contribution to developing the business.

Figure 5
The revised organization structure for the textile company

	Chief executive	Marketing	Manufacturing	Finance	Product development	Yarn purchasing
Business area 1						
Business area 2						
Business area 3						
Business area 4						
Business area 5						

CONSOLIDATION

As a step in consolidating the new organization each business area manager was asked to prepare a growth budget. This budget for the year ahead focused attention on each product/market segment in which the company had any significant business. The budgets in turn were related to a growth strategy developed for each product/market segment. An information system was then set up and reporting relationships developed to review results against these growth budgets on a cyclical basis. Arrangements were also made to prepare development plans for the areas of the business which had not been covered so far.

THE MAIN INFLUENCE GROUP

A key feature of this change process was the existence of a central core group of people who exerted influence on what the company learned during the course of the programmes. This consisted of the chief executive, the external advisor and the executive director given responsibility for liaising between the groups and the external advisor.

The role of the external advisor covered a number of activities. On the one hand he helped the organization to solve its own problems by making it aware of its organizational processes, of their likely consequences and of techniques for effecting change. He also acted as a link between the various levels of management and the different functions in the organization. Another main task was to provide expert advice on issues concerning the development of the businesses.

During the earlier stages of the project his role was to:

(a) provide the initial educational support
(b) help in identifying the main business areas to be studied
(c) help in selecting the people who should form the fact finding groups
(d) advise on the techniques necessary for diagnosing the company's problems
(e) help the fact finding groups both to develop their ideas and to define problems.

During the planning stage the external advisor assumed the following responsibilities, to:

(a) advise on the planning methodology to be used and on the necessary planning tools
(b) assist the groups to develop and complete their plans
(c) coach both the groups and the individuals forming the groups
(d) help the groups in formulating their ideas on the organizational changes and additional resources required
(e) advise on the preparation of growth and profit budgets for the new business sectors
(f) advise on the controls which should be developed to

support the activities within each of the different business sectors.

The executive director chosen to act as liaison man played a number of important parts in the project:

(a) he had to keep the external advisor fully informed about relevant events in the company
(b) he had to provide feedback on any initiatives taken by the influence group
(c) his ability to make impersonal judgements about the result of any initiatives taken was a crucial factor in the success of the project. Here, his role was to help the planning groups think through their situation, identify the problems that needed to be solved, and develop imaginative solutions to the problems identified.

Perhaps the most important task of both change agents (external and internal) was to help the study and planning groups to develop a questioning approach to many of the established ideas and beliefs about the business that were taken for granted. It was particularly important for both change agents to guard against allowing their own prejudices to interfere with the thinking of the groups.

At the start of the project the chief executive needed to demonstrate support for the steps that were being taken. At the same time he took great pains to ensure that the other executives had the power to accept or reject each subsequent stage of the project. In the later stages of the project he played an increasing part in implementing the plans developed. During the creation of plans, he also contributed significantly by giving a second opinion on some of the suggestions being considered.

ASPECTS OF LEARNING

One of the main features of the programme was that the company concerned and many of the individuals in it had to learn about many different aspects of the business. At an early stage it was important for the senior management group to:

1. gain a common understanding of the full extent of the limitations of the existing lines of business. Initially, this involved sharing existing knowledge, rather than seeking new knowledge
2. identify any business lines currently pursued by the company which could be further developed profitably either with existing resources or those which could be readily acquired
3. establish the requirements for success in each of these newer areas of business identified
4. learn to think differently about the company and to see it as a multi-business company rather than one engaged in a single line of business
5. adapt its behaviour to the changed directions of its business and develop new sets of relationships both externally with new customers and suppliers and internally between different sections of the company.

The company, therefore, had to learn about the new markets it wanted to exploit, about the needs of those markets and about ways in which the company could satisfy these needs with some advantage over competitors. It also had to identify and surmount the many problems which inhibited growth in those market sectors. New standards of quality had to be adopted and the company had to learn to cope with the demands and priorities of different industries.

In addition to this it was also important to learn about the issues involved in affecting major changes in an organization and how these can be handled. It was, therefore, important to become familiar with different forms of organizational structure and to learn something about the different types of relationship which these structures entailed. Managers had to learn to appraise their existing styles of management and to think through for themselves how these styles had to change to fit the new organization required.

An important feature of the programme was the one recognized by the participants as a managed programme of learning. Managers were given training in methods of analysis, techniques, etc and were also helped to think through the key factors on which the future success of the company was likely to depend. Participants in the programme were led to question what they were doing at the time and how they were doing it in the light of the development needs of the company.

Educational support

Managers were introduced to techniques for analysing and assessing a number of aspects of the company's business. Particular attention was paid to techniques for exploring product/market relationships, the financial situation in each business area and the relationships between products and production resources. Each group was then briefed on its fact finding tasks and a time-table was established for the project. The groups were allowed to choose their own system of working, perhaps inevitably the executive director in each group assuming responsibility for the progress of the group.

At an early stage in the programme a number of people had shown an interest in learning more about the effects of organization structure and style of management on company performance. As a result, a meeting of senior executives was called to consider some of the organizational and other characteristics which would possibly lead to a more effective business enterprise. It was generally recognized that the three most important were:

(a) knowing the business
(b) having up to date and realistic strategies and plans for the business
(c) having an appropriate organization structure.

'Knowing the business' was interpreted as meaning that the people playing key roles in running the business should have a good understanding of the needs in the market they were satisfying, who was likely to have these needs, where they were located, how effective the company's products and practices were in satisfying the needs, particularly in relation to competitors, and whether any technological and other changes were taking place in the environment which might influence the needs. It was considered important to know whether the company was engaged in one business or a multiplicity of businesses and also how the company was actually making its money.

Effective strategies and plans were identified as those which were designed to achieve growth and profit objectives for each of the different businesses based on up to date information about which markets and customers to aim for, which products to employ and develop for future use, and how it was hoped to obtain advantage over competitors.

An appropriate organization structure would inevitably depend on matching the production and marketing capabilities of the company to the type, location and needs of present and potential customers. The pros and cons of using a matrix structure were explored. Other aspects identified as being important were effective leadership, communications, decision making, motivation, goal setting, giving orders and control.

These characteristics were then appraised in order to establish the extent to which they already existed in the company and to develop tentative conclusions about any changes to be made.

Perhaps the most important aspect of this session was that it created an awareness of the relevance of the above processes, (ie leadership, communications, etc), for the company. There was also a tendency for executives to question their own styles of management in relation to what they as a group had decided was desirable and how they might modify this in group sessions.

For the first time employees began to question whether their activities made any real contribution to company profits. They began to develop ideas on how they could rationalize the company's product range. The chief executive was particularly pleased at this stage because he considered that people were beginning to tackle some of the more fundamental problems of the company which had been neglected in the past.

Follow up review

After a period of some months a review was made of the changes which had taken place and the effects they were having on the company and people. In particular, the review considered what was needed within each business area and at the corporate level to reinforce the learning about how to be more successful as a business. This raised a number of issues, problems and queries, the first of which was the preparation of accounts to show the business groups how well they were doing. Some steps had been taken earlier to make the management accounting information more relevant to the true nature of the business but these modifications had not been sufficient to help the business areas to direct their developments effectively.

A number of organizational issues were also identified. An important one was the need to reconsider and define the role of the chief executive in the planning process. It was evident that he was the lynchpin and had to take responsibility for motivating future planning. He had to recognize and accept the responsibility for helping the business area managers to learn how to run their business and to identify and develop their own roles in this task. It was also apparent that he would need to devote effort to stimulate progress, help to identify priorities of product development and assist the heads of the business areas to develop more effective business ideas. It was further recognized that during the transition stage to a new type of organization no one else could really play this part.

The review also helped to develop a greater insight into the personal learning requirements of the people appointed to the new position of business area managers. Briefly, these were:

(a) to broaden their outlook and accept greater involvement in product development
(b) to focus attention on developing more effective ways of making money in each business area
(c) to learn how to make a better contribution to product development by indicating market needs and by making

potential customers aware of all the capabilities of the new products.

A number of instances indicated that the new organization was still not properly understood. For example, the role of the newly formed development committee was unclear and it was evident that it would take time to establish an identity and to formalize its working relationships with the rest of the company. However, the meetings between the chief executive and the representatives of each business area were seen to be serving very useful purposes and becoming increasingly effective. People were looking ahead rather than spending too much of their time attempting to rehash past developments. The comment was made that 'the new organization has enabled us to make a very favourable impact on a major potential customer'.

Some of the main barriers to growth identified during the review indicated that the company's businesses were beginning to be viewed in a more realistic way. This was illustrated by such observations as:

(a) our existing machinery now needs to be modified to handle a wider range of yarn
(b) we must develop plans for exploiting our new product developments fully
(c) we must carry out experiments to explore business development opportunities which exist with fibres not presently receiving attention
(d) we must try to overcome the lack of capacity at the dyeing and finishing stage which is slowing up the response to product development needs
(e) developments in a particular sales region can be speeded by allocating the sales force more effectively
(f) the product development process is too slow since no one is integrating the various activities involved; this situation must be resolved.

These issues were discussed at length with the chief executive and where possible agreement was reached on a resulting course of action which would be adopted.

Company achievements

At the time of the last review the key people in the company were conscious that they had created a new and flexible organization in which the responsibility for making profits was more widely distributed throughout the management team. It was no longer left simply to the chief executive as in the past. Moreover, people were welcoming the increased responsibility and were consciously planning to improve the profit position. Initiatives, and ideas for worthwhile changes, were being developed throughout the organization, and people were more aware of the options open to the company. New opportunities were being sought to a degree that did not exist in the past. It is probably true to say that the organization was more entrepreneurial than was the case earlier. However, all this was being done within an environment which was becoming increasingly difficult in that the demand for apparel fabrics, their main source of revenue, had shrunk dramatically.

Senior managers were becoming aware that a process had been established for changing the company's strategies and structure more easily which enabled them to deal more effectively with the opportunities and threats generated by the changing business environment.

Personal achievements

People were becoming conscious of the increased freedom of action that the revised organization and planning procedure provided. Those involved in the exercise had gained in experience and knowledge and had increased their personal marketability. They were also being allowed to play a more dynamic role in the development of the company and became more aware of their own and others' contribution to company success. They were becoming more committed to the objectives of the enterprise as a result of having a greater say in some of those decisions on which the company's survival and future growth depended. Since more of them, particularly in middle management, were being brought into contact with the realities of the market place and with the changes taking place in other parts of the business environment, they were more willing to accept any modifications to the organization structure and working practices which were found to be necessary. All these factors helped to make their work more important and encouraged them to participate more fully in the company's activities.

Because of the revised organization structure, a form of matrix based on a number of different semi-autonomous businesses, there were many more opportunities for people to learn about running a business. Whereas before only the chief executive could see all aspects of the company's business, many more personnel were now in a position to understand the totality of a business and to acquire business judgment. They could also better appreciate the need for the company's various functional activities to work in unison.

Conclusion

What had emerged was an organization which had learned:

(a) that the business environment in which it existed was relatively unstable and more subject to both rapid and significant changes affecting profitability and performance than was appreciated at the beginning of the exercise
(b) that more resources needed to be devoted to scanning this environment continually to obtain the information needed to identify and evaluate the new opportunities and threats created by the changes taking place
(c) to adopt a more participative system of planning and decision making which encouraged a speedier formulation of strategies and plans for coping with the changes
(d) to develop a more flexible organization structure which could be modified to implement the new strategies decided on
(e) to encourage a larger number of people to exercise their creative and entrepreneurial talents in project teams engaged in the development of 'whole' businesses. These

people were also given the chance of getting involved in the risk taking that this involved and provided them with the necessary information about the company to help them to do this
(f) to give a greater number of people the opportunity to exercise and develop their individual capabilities.

This is not to say that the organization which had been developed was without faults. In fact, many of the organizational changes which had been introduced created further problems which needed attention. There was still some confusion about 'who' was responsible for 'what'. Many of the prevailing information and control systems were no longer appropriate. For example, the management accounts were still attuned to the earlier organization rather than the new one and stock control systems were still geared to a 'one-type business' rather than a 'multi-business' business.

An important drawback at the time of the last detailed review was that many of the newly introduced practices were still too new to have become part of the company's habitual behaviour. For this reason there was a danger that the company would revert to its earlier set of practices. However, top management was aware of this problem and was taking steps to ensure that the planning and problem-solving processes which had been introduced would become an accepted part of the company's future behaviour.

Perhaps the most significant change in the company was that it had begun to recognize explicitly that its business success was dependent on its ability to learn to cope with new situations. Not only was it important to learn about new needs in the market place and how to satisfy them profitably, but also how to make better use of its more traditional business activities. Moreover, the company was adopting a participative process of planning which it was beginning to recognize as an effective means for obtaining the necessary learning and for ridding itself of myths and beliefs which were no longer justified. In other words, the company was 'learning how to manage its own learning'.

9
Initiating the change process

Every chief executive knows that the popular image of a man who only has to have an idea for his staff to be willing and eager to implement it, is a far cry from reality. Experience shows that the room for manoeuvre on the part of chief executives in getting those things done which they wish to happen is extremely limited. People appear to have an infinite capacity for agreeing verbally and then doing little or nothing. Getting something started is indeed the most difficult part of the whole process of change. This is particularly true where a shared awareness of the need for change is missing.

For the chief executive this implies thinking about the realities of the company's situation, and about its belief and power systems. He could ask himself some of the following questions:

1 Is the company out of tune with its business environment to an extent which might jeopardize its chances of survival?
2 Do subordinates, particularly those in a position of power, fail to perceive the extent of the problem?
3 Are their beliefs and myths about the company's situation significantly out of touch with reality?
4 Is there a lack of consensus about what steps the company should take in order to secure the future?

5 Are there power groups in the company determined to maintain the 'status quo' even at the expense of the company's welfare?

If the answer to some or all of these questions is in the affirmative, then he is confronted with a particularly difficult task in initiating a process of change.

The next step is to think about the areas in which the organization may be out of tune with its environment. Initially this may be the result of a 'gut' feeling, unsupported by real evidence, but significant enough for the chief executive to want to take further action. Perhaps thinking about the gap between myths and reality is a good starting point for initiating it.

The next step is to discuss his ideas with one or more key figures in the organization. One of these should be the person who will be the internal change agent. Choosing the 'right' man for this role is a key decision.

Between them they may decide that an external catalyst may be needed. Who he should be, the role he should play and the amount of time he should be asked to devote to the company are decisions to be taken early because an external change agent, if he is to be effective, needs to be present from the beginning. Perhaps there is only one word of warning: don't choose anyone who wants to work full-time. An external agent's job is to stimulate thinking and that is a part-time role. Change will take place only if a company's own people want it and are willing to learn from the experiences they undergo in making change effective. No external advisor, however competent, can provide a substitute for the efforts of one's own staff, as the previous chapter explained.

WIDENING THE PROCESS

Having identified and made explicit the major areas for concern about the company the next step is to widen the group of people drawn into the change process. These will be senior managers who may or may not immediately recognize that there are major issues affecting the company which indicate conclusively that it is out of touch with its present day environment.

This process can take place in a number of ways, ranging from individual discussions to a weekend away from the company to discuss major problem areas. The methodology is less important than the recognition of the need to find a means of leading people from the views and beliefs they currently hold to a position where *they have convinced themselves* that there is a need for further action. Telling them, using a flip chart covered with facts, bringing in an outsider to convince them and other similar methods are of little avail. What is needed is a means of asking the questions which will inevitably lead this group to recognize through their own efforts that something more needs to be done. The external change agent ought to be able to help to frame the sort of questions which need to be asked.

APPRAISING THE CURRENT SITUATION

This is the stage concerned with establishing 'where are we now?' It is the step which is concerned with putting to the test the initial concerns of the chief executive. Were his hunches justified? Is the company really out of tune with the environment, and if so are the key mismatches in the areas originally identified?

This is also the stage to consider whether certain areas of a well established business might usefully be given more independence so that the people involved are allowed and encouraged to establish what they need to do to harmonize their particular potential with the realities of the market place.

It should now be possible to form teams to collect facts and to examine their implications. The work of the teams can be divided into four aspects:

1 Scanning the environment

This means identifying the various individuals, groups or organizations to which the company directly relates. For example, these could include suppliers, customers, competitors, shareholders, national and local governments, etc. Then establish whether these relationships are stable and equally rewarding to both sides or whether there is an imbalance between what these interest groups give and receive. It also involves establishing whether or not any social, economic, political or technological changes have occurred or are likely to take place which will present opportunities or threats to the company. Some of this work might be subcontracted to a market research company, or outside specialists could be invited to explore special areas such as politics, social responsibility, technology and so on. However, if outsiders are invited to help, their briefing needs to be exact. Any sloppiness will only result in wasted money and poor results.

2 Examining the areas of business

Examination of each of the areas of business being considered is essential in order to identify the key factors for success. This is reasonably straightforward if the previous step has been carried out conscientiously.

3 Identifying mismatches

Identify mismatches between what is required for success and what is actually happening in relation to:

(a) the market segments in terms of the market share already achieved and what increase is feasible in relation to the competition
(b) whether the resources being applied are sufficient or relevant to the needs of the market
(c) whether the way the resources are being used is appropriate.

4 Determining what needs to be done for success

Determine what needs to be done if success is to be achieved for each segment of the business being considered. A judgment is required as to the likelihood of success in relation to the resources and skills which will eventually be available.

While the teams are collecting and assessing the significance of the data, the primary change agents (chief executive and his team) might usefully attempt to identify the main causes of resistance to change. They should consider how the fact finding activities and subsequent planning phase can be used to help overcome this inertia.

> For example, the management accountant in the textile company had been reluctant to act on requests to change the type of information he was producing for management. However, his experiences as a member of one of the fact finding teams soon convinced him that the information he was producing, although correct in terms of management accounting practice, did not help much in developing the business. He therefore established a plan for himself aimed at making the information he produced more relevant to the management of the business.

PLANNING FOR THE FUTURE

This is the stage concerned with determining 'where do we want to be?' at some future date and deciding on 'how best to get there'. When the various teams have reported their findings the stage is set to plan for the future. It is useful for each team to report verbally in the presence of the other groups. This provides a forum for constructive criticism and exchange of ideas. It will also provide reassurance in the sense that each team will discover that the problems it encountered were similar to the experience of the other groups. Important learning can thus take place which will help to lessen resistance to change because the group as a whole will be moving forward.

Planning for the future takes place in three stages:

(a) developing a vision of the future/determining future goals
(b) choosing which of the available options are to be pursued
(c) deciding how to pursue them.

Choosing the options depends on an analysis of:

(a) will the option make a significant impact on business profitability?
(b) have we the skills/knowledge/resources available to make success a reasonable probability?
(c) is success likely within a reasonable time span?

In the early stages it is important to choose one option which will pay off within three months. Too long a lead time before success is achieved can result only in frustration and a lessening of enthusiasm and commitment.

Organizing the work

The objectives now need to be translated into specific work tasks and standards of accomplishment. These tasks should be allocated to individuals and each task should have a time frame for achievement.

This will probably involve some consideration of how work is organized. During the investigation stage informal organizational links will have been developed which will have been at variance with the standard organization chart. The time may now have arrived to decide how much of this informal organization that has developed through the fact finding and planning stages should be accepted for the future. It is worth appreciating that in general organizational change is most effective when it comes after, and not before, changes in work patterns. Many changes in organization fail to achieve their aims because this simple concept is ignored.

> We trained hard – but it seemed that every time we were beginning to form up into teams, we would be reorganized. I was to learn later in life that we tend to meet any new situation by reorganizing, and a wonderful method it can be for creating the illusion of progress while producing confusion, inefficiency and demoralization.
> From Petronii Arbitri Satyricon, AD 66
> attributed to Gaius Petronius.

Managing the transition

This stage is concerned with making the transition from 'where we are now' to 'where we want to be'. Naturally it is important to set up systems for reviewing the attainment of the plans. Responsibility for their translation into practice will have been given and the necessary resources allocated. The focus should be on providing information and control data which will support the development of each business area, rather than on 'looking over the manager's shoulder'. A good maxim is that 'self-control is the best form of control'. A key question to ask those who are given responsibility is 'how will you know if you are succeeding?' It is impossible to answer this question without detailed consideration of how the plans translate into practice.

Regular review of the plans provides ample learning opportunity. Perhaps the most important objective of the review process is to produce an organization which is continuously improving its competence in coping with a changing business environment.

What can be achieved

The character of the company which could emerge as a result of the above process could be appreciably different from the one which existed at the outset. If the new organization is to work well, and to react quickly to change, many new internal relationships will have had to be formed. There will need to be greater understanding of the roles of others and closer liaison between sections of the business which did not previously recognize the need for working together. In short, an organization could well have been created which is vibrant rather than ossified; prepared to modify its entrenched views rather than defend existing stances; above all, one in which managers will recognize that they have a substantial and exciting personal contribution to make to the well-being of the business.

Provided the process has been properly managed, the outcome will be an organization which has a better understanding of the present day needs of that part of society which constitutes its environment and of how these needs are changing. There will also be plans for satisfying these needs subject to the limitation of available resources.

An organization should have been created in which responsibility for developing the various existing and potential businesses in the company in terms of both strategy and tactics is allocated to a number of people at lower levels than before. Many people should appreciate, perhaps for the first time in their careers, that they are contributing to a business rather than merely carrying out their functional responsibilities. It could be an organization in which the leader's role may have changed significantly; perhaps from one of being the main driving force behind the company's businesses to one in which he may be the main support to a number of other managers driving smaller businesses. In this case a main part of his role would be to agree the growth and profit objectives with the people running these businesses. He would also arbitrate between the various businesses, particularly in relation to allocating additional resources. He would ensure that each main business and other areas of activity have a management and structure which can cope with the problems of efficient operation and future development.

Strategic management

So far this book has discussed the steps which need to be taken to set in motion a process which will enable a company to achieve a state of congruence with its environment.

Thought now needs to be given to what is required to ensure that the organization is capable of keeping in tune with its environment in the future. This task can be described as the 'strategic management' of a company. It is represented in figure 6 on page 131 by a fourth circle which ensures that the factors represented by the other three circles are kept in tune. It may consist of a single individual, in which case he must be the person who almost certainly wields greater power than anyone else in the company. Alternatively, it may consist of a small group of people which must also contain a key figure in the power structure, for example, the chief executive and perhaps the internal change agents.

Figure 6

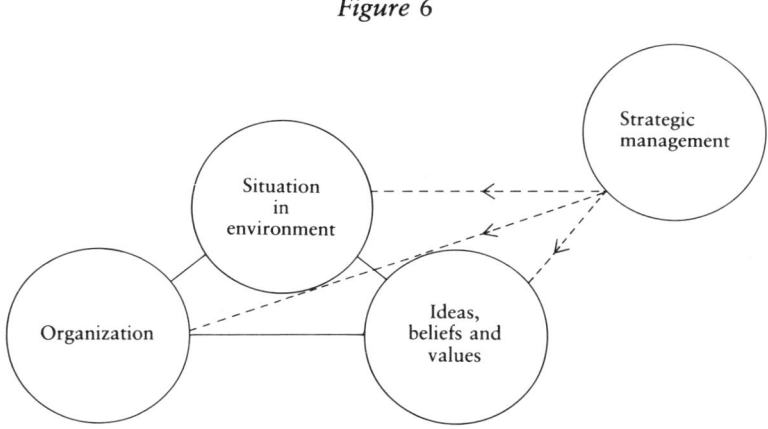

It can be considered as that aspect of management which creates and maintains a climate in which appropriate changes can be made, and initiates those actions which will lead to the desired changes actually taking place.

Some of the main components of the task of *'strategic management'* should be as follows:

(a) To maintain an appropriate balance between the company's various established and developing businesses. A balance needs to be struck between new lines of business which are still in the course of development and are consumers of finance, with more mature lines which are well established and are generating more funds than they actually need to maintain themselves. These two types of business should complement each other and ensure that a company can be adequately profitable although its various businesses might be at various stages of growth or degeneration.

(b) To regulate and modify the company's system of ideas, beliefs and values in order to ensure that these take account of relevant environmental changes and prevent the company from becoming trapped by out of date

concepts or ideas. This may require the generation and maintenance of a tension between differing ideas about what is required for longer term success in the company.
(c) To decide how the company should change, eg diversification, with new ideas or businesses to develop, etc.
(d) To manage the company's learning in a way that enables the company to continue to cope with changing circumstances.

Perhaps the most important task is to see that the company has a satisfactorily functioning internal political system (ie a system which redistributes power, status and resources). This is a necessary condition for ensuring that the organization remains sufficiently flexible to accomplish appropriate adaptation in a company faced with major structural changes in its environment.

A characteristic of 'strategic management' is that it recognizes the importance of having a deep understanding of the ways in which businesses can be created and helped to grow through various stages until a high degree of maturity and market dominance have been achieved.

It should not be the role of 'strategic management' to get involved in the problems of individual businesses or operations, other than to assess and comment on their overall performance. Rather it should act more by influencing the organization structure, the power system and the mechanisms for resolving conflicts in the company. This could include for example:

(a) bringing conflicting ideas held by different members in the main power group together in order to achieve some form of synergy
(b) modifying the company's problem-solving capabilities, ie increasing problem-solving resources
(c) changing values by introducing new incentives and rewards
(d) making changes to the planning and control systems
(e) influencing the company's system of ideas, beliefs and values
(f) adjusting the resource allocation system so that the

various lines of business are subjected to new demands and conditions.

It has been said that 'strategic management' is not concerned with intervening in the game itself, rather it exerts influence mainly by changing the rules and plan of the game. In order to be fully effective it should exert the necessary control over the implementation of its plans more by getting other people to grow and develop rather than by the direct exercise of power.

Requirements of efficient 'strategic management'

In order to be fully effective 'strategic management' needs the following:

1 A good feel for internal political processes and tensions.
2 An understanding of the structure of the wider social system to which the company and its industry belongs and how this structure is changing.
3 A mental picture of the company, its various lines of business and its relationship with its environment which accords with reality, together with a vision of a required future state, which can be used to assess the likely impact of internal and external changes on the organization and to develop ideas on the form of action to take to achieve the vision.
4 The means to influence the organization structure, ie the power system, conflict resolving mechanisms, the cognitive system, control systems, etc in order to change the company's ability to grow or to cope with its environment which may be in course of change.
5 An understanding of the contribution that both individual and organizational learning can make to the task of coping with a changing environment and the knowledge of how the company's learning can be managed in order to improve organizational competence.
6 The ability to identify and remove the various retardants which can inhibit the processes leading to necessary

changes in the system of ideas and beliefs. This will include satisifying genuine staff and management development needs, determining additional requirements for staff and special skills, and deciding how future organizational and individual learning within the company should be developed.

Provided that the top management of a company, supported by whatever additional change agents are thought to be necessary, are capable of meeting these requirements, then there is a good chance of maintaining a 'successful' company. In other words, of having a company which is capable of modifying its:

1 perception of its internal and external situations
2 philosophies and organizational structures
3 definition of its role and mission
4 strategies, plans, resources and actions

in accordance with the demands of any new situation with which it is confronted by its changing business environment.

APPENDIX

Getting to know the business and its problems

PART I

Listed below are a set of questions the answers to which should assist management to develop a sound understanding of its company's business or businesses. They will also help to highlight significant mismatches both between and within the groups of factors which go to make up:

A the company's environment
B its organization
C its system of ideas, beliefs and values.

A THE COMPANY'S ENVIRONMENT

1 The primary environment – relevant interest groups

(a) Which organizations, groups and individuals have a direct interest in the company, such as customers, personnel, etc?
(b) How do the contributions made by the interest groups

compare with the rewards or benefits they receive and what key mismatches exist between the two, particularly for customers and suppliers?
(c) How important are the interest groups to the organization? How significant are the mismatches identified?

2 Secondary environment

(a) Which are the people, groups and organizations whose judgement of the company's performance can affect the company to any appreciable extent, eg financial press, investors, money market, potential customers, etc?
(b) What criteria of evaluation do they use and what demands do they make on the company?
(c) What mismatches exist between the demands made on the company and the extent to which the demands are satisfied in terms of the criteria of evaluation?

3 The future environment

(a) What significant developments are taking place in sections of the environment of the company such as work, housing, leisure, communications, technology, patterns of consumption, education, transportation, politics, society, etc?
(b) In which direction and to what extent are these trends likely to take place, in particular what major changes in new needs, resources, values, etc?
(c) Which new mismatches, problems or opportunities are likely to be created by these changes?

4 Product/market relationship

(a) Who are the customers and how can they be segmented into useful groups, eg on the basis of different industries or different end uses or geographical locations, etc?
(b) How can the products be grouped in relation to the kind of customer needs being satisfied?
(c) Prepare one or more product/market matrices making use of the classifications estabished in (a) and (b) above.

(d) Withing each product/market segment establish:
   (i) the income generated
   (ii) profit or contribution
   (iii) market share of the company
   (iv) total size of market
   (v) vulnerability to competitors, technological change or changes in customer needs
   (vi) growth potential – where is growth restricted
   (vii) who are the main competitors and what are their strengths and weaknesses in relation to the company
   (viii) who is the market segment leader, why has he been successful
   (ix) what investment is needed for further growth in the segment
   (x) the company's competitive advantage (if any) in each segment.
(e) From which market segments does the company obtain most of its business and profits and which other segments would justify further effort?
(f) Which key mismatches exist between the real needs in each market segment and the properties or qualities of the products or services provided?
(g) Within each market segment establish:
   (i) who is the purchaser and why is he buying from you
   (ii) what is the purchaser actually buying ie, what need is he satisfying
   (iii) where is the buying decision made and how is the decision reached.
(h) Which product/market segments provide the greatest opportunities?

5 Suppliers to the company

(a) What are the company's main purchases and who are the main suppliers?
(b) How dependent is the company on various types of materials and suppliers?

(c) Does the company dominate any supplies of raw materials?
(d) Which mismatches exist between the demands of the suppliers and the way in which the company meets these demands?
(e) How important are aspects of the supply situation to the company's 'business idea(s)'?

B THE ORGANIZATION

1 The production processes

(a) What is the process of production (prepare this in chart form)? What are the main input components and materials and the essential stages in the process?
(b) What are the main interdependencies between:
  (i) products and stages of production
  (ii) various lines of production and production operations
  (iii) markets, products and production units
  (iv) various products.
(c) What are the capacities of the various departments and how are they being utilized? Where do spare capacity or bottlenecks exist – how can capacity be expanded?
(d) What is the structure of manufacturing costs?
(e) How is production organized in relation to the various products and where do mismatches exist?

2 Organization structure and administration

(a) To what extent is the company's top management group aware of the fact that significant changes need to be made – what degree of consensus is there about what should be done?
(b) What resources are used for long range planning or for new developments in products or methods of working?

(c) What and how effective are the company's methods for handling the relationships with the main interest groups, eg sales and sales promotion, personnel, administration, etc?
(d) How is marketing and selling organized?
(e) How and how well is production controlled and related to customers' needs?
(f) How is quality controlled?
(g) How are resources allocated to business areas and markets – is this allocation more consistent with the past situation rather than to future prospects?
(h) Where do mismatches occur between what the company is trying to do and its administration and organization structure?

3 Financial position

(a) Over the last five or 10 years, establish what has been the:
- (i) total working capital employed in various parts of the business
- (ii) profit – before taxes and interest charges
- (iii) sales income
- (iv) profit margins
- (v) turnover of total working capital
- (vi) return on working capital
- (vii) owners' equity
- (viii) turnover of owners' equity
- (ix) return on owners' equity.

(b) Plot how the return on working capital and owners equity have varied over the years and evaluate the company's ability to use money productively.
(c) Forecast the company's sales and capital requirements for the next five years.
(d) Ascertain what might be done to improve the company's return on capital and owners equity employed by either –
- (i) increasing the rate of capital turnover
- (ii) increasing the margin on each turnover of working capital.

(e) Assess whether the future available finance is consistent with the company's growth expectations.
(f) Assess the extent to which financial resources are being allocated so as to maximise expected returns.

C The company's value system

(a) What can be determined about the key aspects of the company's system of values (ie what is considered important) by a review of existing policies and practices and the system of rewards and punishments? How relevant are these things to the company's present needs and ambitions?
(b) What are the main areas of the business – are these mutually consistent; why does the company exist (ie mission); what is it doing to satisfy those aims (role), and how well are these aims being met.
(c) What are the objectives and goals of the company in relation to growth and performance – are they realistic – how well are they being satisfied.

D Environment/organization/values – interrelationships

(a) What is/are the company's business(es) – ie in what ways does the company make its money.
(Define these in terms of markets, products, supporting organizations and services and special competence or competitive advantage).
(b) At what stage of growth are the businesses (ie an interesting idea, in course of development, established but increasing its penetration of the market place, mature or decaying) and are they capable of further profitable growth.
(c) Are the objectives and development plans for each business consistent with its stage of growth
(d) Are the company's objectives and plans for achieving them particularly in the longer term, realistic in relation

to the whole portfolio of businesses and the likely future availability of resources.

PART II

From the answers to the above questions the ideas for changing the company's strategies, organization and action plans should begin to emerge.

In particular they should enable the following issues to be addressed more effectively:

(a) in which directions should the company grow
(b) how should resources best be re-allocated in relation to markets and to product groups
(c) what strategies should be adopted and actions taken in order to solve the main problems and rectify the key mismatches affecting the company's performance and growth prospects.

Bibliography

ABERNATHY W J *and* WAYNE, K *Limits of the Learning Curve.* Harvard Business Revue, Sept/Oct, 1974 pp 109–119.

ACKOFF, Russel L *A Concept of Corporate Planning.* Wiley-Interscience, 1970.

ADAIR, John *Action-centred Leadership.* Farnborough, Hants, Gower Press, Teakfield Ltd, 1979.

ANSOFF, H I *Corporate Strategy.* McGraw Hill, 1965 New York.

ANSOFF, H Igor *Ed. Business Strategy.* Penguin Books, 1969.

ARGENTI, John *Corporate Collapse: The Causes and Symptoms.* Maidenhead, Berks., McGraw Hill, 1976.

ARGENTI, John *Systematic Corporate Planning.* London, Thomas Nelson, 1974.

ARGYRIS, Chris. *Integrating the Individual and the Organisation.* John Wiley and Sons Inc, 1964.

ARGYRIS, Chris *and* SCHON, Donald A *Organizational Learning: A Theory of Action Perspective.* Reading, Mass, Addison-Wesley, 1978.

ARGYRIS, Chris *and* SCHON, Donald A *Theory in Practice: Increasing Professional Effectiveness.* Jossey-Bass Publishers, 1976.

BARTLETT & KEYSER *Changing Organisational Behaviour.* Prentice Hall, 1973.

BASIL, Douglas C *and* COOK, Curtis W *The Management of Change.* Maidenhead, Berks., McGraw Hill, 1974.

BEARD, Ruth *Teaching and Learning in Higher Education.* Penguin Books, 1976.

BENNIS, Warren G *Organization Development: Its Nature, Origins, and Prospects.* Reading, Mass, Addison-Wesley, 1969.

BENNIS, Warren G *et al The Planning of Change.* 2nd ed, London, Holt, Rinehart & Winston, 1970.

BEVERIDGE, W I B *The Art of Scientific Investigation.* Mercury Books No. 13, 1964.

BLUMBERG, A and GOLEMBIEWSKI, R T *Learning and Change in Groups.* Penguin Books, 1976.

BURNS, T and STALKER, G M *The Management of Innovation.* Tavistock, London, 1961.

BURTON, John W *Conflict and Communication.* London, Macmillan, 1969.

BUZAN, Tony *Use Your Head.* London, British Broadcasting Corporation, 1974.

CHANDLER, Alfred D *Strategy and Structure: Chapters in the History of the Industrial Enterprise.* Cambridge, Massachusetts Institute of Technology, 1962.

CHILD, John *Organization: A Guide to Problems and Practice.* London, Harper & Row, 1977.

CLARK, Peter A *Organisational Design.* Tavistock, 1972.

CYERT, R M and MARCH, J G *A Behavioral Theory of the Firm.* Prentice-Hall, Englewood Cliffs, NJ.

DALTON, LAWRENCE & GREINER *Organisational Change and Development.* Irwin-Dorsey, 1970.

DAVIES, I K *The Management of Learning.* McGraw Hill, 1971.

DRUCKER, Peter E *Management, Tasks, Responsibilities, Practices.* Heinemann – London, 1974.

DRUCKNER, Peter F *New Templates for Today's Organisations.* Harvard Business Revue, Jan/Feb, 1974, pp. 45–53.

DYER, William G *Team Building: Issues and Alternatives.* Reading, Mass, Addison-Wesley, 1977.

ELLIOTT, John *Conflict or Co-operation? The Growth of Industrial Democracy.* London, Kogan Page, 1978.

EMERY, F E and TRIST, E L *The Causal Texture of Organizational Environments.* Hum. Rel., 18. 1, pp. 21–23. (Also pub in EMERY, F E *Ed. Systems Thinking.* Penguin, Harmondsworth, Middlesex).

FLETCHER, John *How to Write a Report* I P M January, 1983.

FRANKL, Victor E *Mans Search for Meaning.* Hodder & Stroughton, 1964.

GALBRAITH, Jay R and NATHANSON, Daniel A *Strategy Implementation: The Role of Structure & Process.* West Publishing Co, 1978.

HACON, Richard *Ed. Personal and Organizational Effectiveness.* Maidenhead, Berks., McGraw Hill, 1972.

HANDY, Charles B. *Understanding Organisations.* Harmondsworth, Middlesex, Penguin Books, 1976.

HARGREAVES, John *and* DAUMAN, Jan *Business Survival and Social Change: A Practical Guide to Responsibility and Partnership.* London, Associated Business Programmes, 1975.

HEIRS, Ben *and* PEHRSON, Gordon *The Mind of the Organisation.* Harper and Row, 1982.

HIRSCHMANN, W B *Profit From the Learning Curve* Harvard Business Revue, Jan/Feb. 1964.

HONEY, Peter *Face to Face: A Practical Guide to Interactive Skills.* London, Institute of Personnel Management, 1976.

HUNT, John W *Managing People at Work: A Manager's Guide to Behaviour in Organizations.* Maidenhead, Berks., McGraw Hill, 1979.

HUSSEY, D F *Introducing Corporate Planning.* 2nd edn Oxford, Pergamon Press, 1979.

INSTITUTE OF PERSONNEL MANAGEMENT *The human Face of Change: Social Responsibility and Rationalisation at British Steel* by Ken Jones. London, Institute of Personnel Management, 1974.

INSTITUTE OF PERSONNEL MANAGEMENT *Managing Change – A Strategy for Our time* by Hugh Marlow. London, Institute of Personnel Management, 1975

INSTITUTE OF PERSONNEL MANAGEMENT *OD: The Search for Identity.* London, The Institute of Personnel Management, 1974.

INSTITUTE OF PERSONNEL MANAGEMENT *Personnel in Change: Organization Development through the Personnel Function* ed by Thakur *et al,* London, The Institute of Personnel Management, 1978.

INSTITUTE OF PERSONNEL MANAGEMENT *Worker Participation: Individual Control and Performance* by David Guest and Derek Fatchett. London, Institute of Personnel Management, 1974.

JAY, Anthony *Effective Presentation: The Communication of Ideas by Words and Visual Aids.* London, Management Publications, 1970.

JOHNSTON, A V *Organisation Development and the Natural Process of Change and its Management.* Accountancy Age, 1976.

JUN, J S *and* STORM, W B *Tomorrow's Organisations – Challenges and Strategies* Scott, Foresimen and Co, 1973.

JUNG, C G *The Undiscovered Self* Routledge & Kegan Paul, 1974.

KEMPNER, Thomas *et al Business and Society: Tradition and Change.* London, Allen Lane at the Penguin Press, 1974.

KEPNER, Charles H *and* TREGOE, Benjamin B *The Rational Manager: A Systematic Approach to Problem Solving and Decision-Making*. 2nd edn New Jersey, Princeton, Kepner-Tregoe Inc, 1976.

KINGDOM, R K *Matrix Organisation*. Tavistock, 1973.

KLEIN, Josephine *Working with Groups*. Hutchinson University Library, 1963.

KNIGHT, Kenneth *Ed. Matrix Management*. Farnborough, Hants. Gower Press. Teakfield Ltd, 1977.

KRECH, CRUTCHFIELD & BALLACHEY *The Individual in Society* McGraw Hill, 1962.

KUHN, T S *The Structure of Scientific Revolutions* University of Chicago Press, 1962.

LAWRENCE, P R *The Changing of Organisational Behaviour Patterns* . Harvard University Press, 1958.

LAWRENCE P R *and* LORSCH, J W *Organisation and Environment. Managing Differentation and Integration*. Harvard University Press, 1967.

LEIGH, Andrew *Decisions, Decisions!* I P M January, 1983.

LEVITT, T *Marketing Myopia* Harvard Business Revue, 1960. 38.1.

LIKERT, Rehsis *New Patterns of Management*. McGraw Hill, 1961.

LIKERT, Rehsis *The Human Organisation*. McGraw Hill, 1967.

LIPPITT, Gordon L *Organizational Renewal: Achieving Viability in a Changing World*. New York, Appleton Century Crofts, 1969.

LIPPITT, WATSON, WESTLEY *The Dynamics of Planned Change*. Harcourt, Brase and World Inc, 1958.

MARGERISON, Charles J *Influencing Organizational Change: The Role of the Personnel Specialist*. London, Institute of Personnel Management, 1978.

MARGERISON, Charles J *Managing Effective Work Groups*. Maidenhead, Berks., McGraw Hill, 1973.

MASLOW, Abraham H *Towards a Psychology of Being* D. Van Nostrand, 1968.

MASLOW, Abraham H *Eupsychian Management*. Richard D. Irwin Inc and the Dorsey Press, 1965.

MASLOW, Abraham *Motivation and Behaviour*. Harper and Row, 1970.

MERRY, Uri *and* ALLERHAND, Melvin E *Developing Teams and Organizations: A Practical Handbook for Managers and Consultants*. Reading, Mass, Addison-Wesley, 1977.

MILLER and RICE *Systems of Organisation* Tavistock, 1973.

MUMFORD, Alan *Making Experience Pay: Management Success through Effective Learning.* Maidenhead, Berks., McGraw Hill, 1980.

MUMFORD, Enid and PETTIGREW, Andrew *Implementing Strategic Decisions.* London, Longman, 1975.

NORMANN, R. *Management for Growth.* Wiley, 1977.

NORMANN, Richard *Growth & Learning in Business Organisations – Some Problems and Ideas* S.I.A.R. Documentation AB.

OSBORN, Alex F *Applied Imagination: Principles and Procedures of Creative Thinking.* New York, Charles Scribners's, 1953.

PATTEN, Thomas H *Relating Learning Theory to Behavioural Change in Organisations.* Paper presented at International Training & Development Conference Geneva, October 15–20, 1972.

PEDLAR, Mike et al *A Manager's Guide to Self-Development.* Maidenhead, Berks., McGraw Hill, 1978.

PERROW, C *Organisational Analysis.* Tavistock, 1970.

POOLE, Michael *Workers' Participation in Industry.* London, Routledge & Kegan Paul, 1978.

POPPER, Karl *The Logic of Scientific Discovery.* Hutchinson, 1972.

POPPER, Karl *Conjectures and Refutations, the Growth of Scientific Knowledge.* Routledge and Kegan Paul, 1972.

PORTER, Lyman W and ROBERTS, Karlene H *Communication in Organizations: Selected Readings.* Harmondsworth, Middlesex, Penguin Books, 1977.

PORTER, Michael E *Competitive Strategy: Techniques for Analysing Industries and Competitors.* The Free Press, 1980.

PRIOR, Peter J *Leadership is not a Bowler Hat.* Newton Abbott, Devon. David and Charles, 1977.

RHENMAN, E *Organisation Theory for Long Range Planning.* Wiley, 1973.

RICKARDS, Tudor *Problem Solving through Creative Analysis.* Epping, Essex. Gower Press for British Institute of Management, 1974.

ROEBER, Richard J C *The Organization in a Changing Environment.* Reading, Mass, Addison-Wesley, 1973.

ROGERS, C *Carl Rogers on Personal Power*, Constable, 1977.

RUITENBECK H M Ed. *Psychoanalysis & Existential Philosophy* E P Dutton and Co Inc, 1962.

SATRE, Jean Paul *Existentialism and Humanism.* Eyre Methuen Ltd, 1973.

SCHIEN, Edgar H *Process Consultation: Its Role in Organization Development.* Reading, Mass, Addison-Wesley, 1969.

SCHON, Donald A *Invention and the Evolution of Ideas.* Tavistock Publications, 1963.

SCHUMACHER, E F *Small is Beautiful – A Study of Economics as if People Mattered.* ABACUS, 1975.

SELZNICK, P *Leadership in Administration.* Row, Peterson, Evanston, Ill, 1957.

SHIRLEY, R C *Strategy and Policy Formation – a multifunctional orientation.* John Wiley and Sons Inc. 1976.

SIDNEY, Elizabeth et al *Skills with People: A Guide for Managers.* London, Hutchinson, 1973.

SINGER, Edwin J *Effective Management Coaching.* 2nd edn London, Institute of Personnel Management, 1979.

SOFER, C *Organisations in Theory and Practice* Heinemann, 1972.

SOLOMON, Robert C *Ed. Phenomenoloy and Existentialism.* Harper & Row, 1972.

STYMNE, B. *Values and Processes. A Systems Study of Effectiveness in Three Organizations.* Studenlitteratur, Lund. 1970. (SIAR-17) (Diss.)

TAYLOR, R and SPARKES, J R *Corporate Strategy and Planning.* Heinemann, 1977.

TAYLOR, Derek E *Coping with Change.* Management Today, October, 1977.

TAYLOR, DEREK E *Strategic Planning as an Organisational Change Process – Some Guidelines from Practice.* Long Range Planning, Vol. 12 No. 5.

TOFFLER, Alvin *Future Shock.* Pan Books Ltd, 1973.

WALTON, Richard E *Interpersonal Peacemaking: Confrontations and Third Party Consultation.* Reading, Mass, Addison-Wesley, 1969.

WARMINGTON, Allan et al *Organizational behaviour and performance: An Open Systems Approach to Change.* London, Macmillan, 1977.

WEINSHALL, Theodore D *Managerial Communication: Concepts, Approaches and Techniques.* London, New York, Academic Press, 1979.

WICKES, Frances G *The Inner World of Choice.* Coventure Ltd, London, 1977.

WOODCOCK, Mike *Team Development Manual.* Farnborough, Hants., Gower Press, Teakfield Ltd, 1979.

Index

AEI Ltd 9

BMC (BL) 9

Change
  bringing about 39 *et seq*
  process of 13 *et seq*
Change agents 16, 50, 78, 89 *et seq*
  external 92
  internal 93
  role of 90 *et seq*
  selection of 91
  skills of 93 *et seq*
Companies
  and the environment 18 *et seq*
  establishing present situation 58 *et seq*
  mismatches with environment 23
  power groups in 22, 25
  programmes of learning 42 *et seq*
  system of ideas, beliefs and values 21 *et seq*
  system of values 24 *et seq*

Company
  organization 20 *et seq*
Company systems
  rewards and punishments 74 *et seq*
Consultants
  use of 68
Current situation
  appraisal of 125

De Beers Corporation 59

Educational assistance
  use of 54 *et seq*
Edwardes, Sir Michael 9
Environment
  scanning of 125
Experimentation
  the importance of 40

Industrial Training Research Unit 86
Information
  shortage of 77
  systematization of 96 *et seq*

Kingston Regional Management Centre 54, 69, 81

Learning 3, 63
  differences from training 34
  establishing a company's
    needs 44 *et seq*
  managing a company's 55 *et seq*
  organizational 30 *et seq*
  recognizing a need 43
  to adapt 4
  See also Organizational learning
Learning curves 34 *et seq*
  B-29 plane 35
Learning needs
  of board of directors 52
  of chief executives 52
  of departmental heads 53
  of groups within
    companies 51
  of managers 53
  of staff specialists 53
Listening 97 *et seq*

Management
  by objectives 9
  changes in top 8
  development of 9
Management consultants
  use of 9
Mismatches
  identification of 47, 126

Organization structure 20
  bureaucratic 70
  functional 70
  organic 72
  types of 69 *et seq*
Organizational learning
  evaluation of 49
  examples of 34
  steps in 45 *et seq*

Planner
  role of corporate 67

Planning 78
  corporate 10
  for the future 127 *et seq*
  implementation of 64 *et seq*
  reviews 63 *et seq*
Planning process
  establishment of 80 *et seq*
Problems
  identification of 94

Questioning 98 *et seq*

Rolls Royce 4, 9

Schumacher, P.C. 24
Senior executives
  gaining commitment of 83 *et seq*
Silence
  use of as a skill 101
Stanford Research Institute 34
States of Jersey 79
Strategic management 130 *et seq*
  requirements of 133
Strategic planning 57
Summarizing 100
Systems
  information and control 62 *et seq*

Teams
  development of 85 *et seq*
  leaders of 86
Tensions
  handling of 81 *et seq*
Timex corporation 26, 60

Verbal presentations 101
Visions 66 *et seq*

Weinstock, Sir Arnold 9
Writing persuasively 103